Library of Congress Catalog Card No. 84-63024.

19th Century
French Prints Drawings
& Bronzes

On Cover
Cat. No. 95 JEAN-FRANÇOIS MILLET (1814-1875)

45. DEGAS

Bronze, about 1890-1900

R. S. JOHNSON INTERNATIONAL / 645 NORTH MICHIGAN AVENUE
CHICAGO, ILLINOIS 60611 / TELEPHONE (312) 943-1661

19TH CENTURY FRENCH PRINTS DRAWINGS & BRONZES

APRIL 1985

INTRODUCTION

SOME THOUGHTS
ON 19TH CENTURY FRENCH ART

*

CATALOGUE

*

ADDENDUM

SELECTED NOTES ON THE HISTORY
OF NINETEENTH CENTURY FRANCE

Nota bene

All of the works in this catalogue are either collection of or formerly collection of R.S. Johnson International. To those museums and collectors who generously have been willing to lend back to us works for this exhibition, we should like to express our deep appreciation.

SOME THOUGHTS ON
19TH CENTURY FRENCH ART

Between 1800 and 1900, France was the center of a phenomenal artistic development. The richness of these years becomes clear in considering some of the innovators in the visual arts. These would include : J.L. David, Géricault, Delacroix, Ingres, Courbet, Millet, Daumier, Meryon, Corot, Rodin, Manet, Degas, Pissarro, Renoir, Monet, Cézanne, Seurat, Van Gogh, Henri Rousseau, Redon, Gauguin, Toulouse-Lautrec, Bonnard and Vuillard. This subject is further enlarged by a nineteenth century France which was a fountainhead of cultural achievements. It would not be right to separate a fragment of the history of art of this period from the broad, intellectual milieu in which that art was created. Keeping this in mind, our purpose here is only a modest attempt to present some basic concepts and guidelines for a better understanding of the general context of this exhibition.

*

* *

At the beginning of France's nineteenth century, one artist, Jacques-Louis David (1748-1825) and his school, usually described as «Classicism», dominated the art scene. In the first quarter of the century, the first major challenge to David was made by Théodore Géricault (1791-1824). By 1830, David was outdated and for Eugène Delacroix (1798-1863) : «Michelangelo, antique masks and Géricault» were the elements which «opened infinite horizons and authorized all the new developments». It is surprising today to see how few artists were able to determine the directions of art in these years in France and also to understand how narrow was the basis, at the time, for judging these directions. For instance, at the middle of the century in the salon reviews, only painting was discussed thoroughly by the critics of the day. Drawings, watercolors, prints, book illustrations, even sculpture and architecture were hardly mentioned. However, as France moved brilliantly forward into the nineteenth century, it became inacceptable to isolate one form of art from another and impossible to continue separating one aspect of art from the multitude of other developments in the arts and sciences. The interaction between art and literature was particularly significant. In this respect, a number of writers could be mentioned, including : Balzac, Victor Hugo, Théophile Gautier, Baudelaire, Flaubert, Zola, Mallarmé, Verlaine and Maupassant. For example, Baudelaire, who as a youth spent days at a time wandering among the Paris print dealers and visiting the Cabinet des Estampes in the Louvre, surrounded himself with art objects. A great admirer of Delacroix, whom he considered to be «absolutely the most original artist of past and modern times» (1), as well as of the etchings of Meryon, Baudelaire's writings started with art criticism. Gustave Flaubert, though known today mainly for his *Madame Bovary*, also produced some of the most perceptive, contemporary writing on the new premises of nineteenth century French art and literature. Zola was equally important as a novelist and as the critic who best understood the revolutionary significance of Edouard Manet. Besides literature, it also became less and less acceptable to separate art from many other developments in French culture. Here we would have to mention : Georges Sorel, Tarde and Durkheim for their contributions to the social sciences ; Berthelot, Curie and Pasteur in the pure sciences ; Bizet, Debussy, Massenet and Ravel in music ; Sarah Bernhardt and many others from the world of theater ; and finally at least Auguste Comte and Bergson in philosophy. All this magnificent and inter-related cultural flowering came to an abrupt halt after the outbreak of World War I in 1914.

(1) Page 14 of : Baudelaire : *Curiosités Esthétiques*, 1968 Paris edition.

In nineteenth century France, one can see a gradual change from what could be called «traditional art» to what might be called «modern art». The steps in this development have been rather questionably placed in neat categories labeled : «Classicism» (J.L. David) ; «Romanticism» (Géricault, Delacroix) ; «Realism» (Courbet) ; «Pure Painting» (Manet, Degas and the impressionists who followed) and «Post-Impressionism» (Gauguin, Toulouse-Lautrec). Other criss-crossing categories have been established under such titles as : «Conservatism», «Humanitarianism», «Objectivism», «Positivism», «Naturalism» and «Symbolism». The limitations of such categorizing could be illustrated by the relationship of Delacroix, perhaps the best known «Romantic», with «Romanticism». One of the eventual objectives of this latter movement would appear to have been the creation of a newer and more broadly based form of «Classicism». This objective could partially explain Delacroix's «lapses», late in his career, into «history painting». These «lapses» could be called a «new» form of «Classicism» ; they also could be described as merely a return to the «old» Classicism of J.L. David. (2) Another element, in which category lines could appear confusing, concerns the importance which Delacroix accorded to technique and originality. This emphasis by Delacroix was very close to «pure painting» and the future ideas of Manet. Still another confusion results from a modern analysis of nineteenth century art. In this respect we now tend to accord more weight to Delacroix's style and less to his subject matter. In 1830, however, Delacroix's work was seen with much more subject-matter orientated eyes. In conclusion, like all great creators, Delacroix, in time and substance, constantly transgresses limiting categories.

Whatever categories might be established, there is no doubt that at the beginning of the nineteenth century in France, literary sources, historical and religious events from the distant past or more contemporary times formed the basis for a great ensemble called «historical painting». This type of painting, both for the critics and the public, represented the then most acceptable form of art. Reflected by the success of the artist of the moment, J.L. David, historically orientated subject matter was not only considered superior to other subject matters but, in addition, other artists, through their choice of other subjects, were by that fact alone declared to be inferior. Thus, in late eighteenth and early nineteenth century France, painterly qualities and «style» were sublimated to the choice of subject matter. (3)

In the period immediately following David, «kings and heroes, gods and saints» (4) began to be put aside and man himself and his condition became the concern of the leading artists. This new art, called «Romanticism», extended from about 1798 until 1847. Conceived originally as a reaction against «Classicism» (either Greco-Roman or French), one of Romanticism's strivings was an attempt to reject the «hierarchy of genres». In this hierarchy, as we pointed out, «history painting» had been established as superior to landscape, still life and interior scenes. The artist, with whom we associate the beginning of Romanticism in France, is Géricault. In examining Géricault's *Return from Russia*, 1818 (Fig. 1, cat. no. 65), for example, we see no indication of the identity of the two soldiers in question nor do we see a specific historical moment. We also have not been presented with a general retreat from a given battle-scene but only with a fragment of this retreat. In this fragment, the two soldiers appear to symbolize the thousands of defeated and wounded soldiers returning from Napoléon's ill-fated thrust into Russia. These two soldiers are only «marginal» aspects of a more general situation, «marginal» aspects which, contrary to a more «classical» presentation, are given the same importance as would be given to say the depiction of Napoléon himself or to a view of a whole army in retreat. This emergence of the «marginal» and the gradual elimination of the concept of centrality in art was a basic characteristic of the Romantic movement. Romantic theory called for a destruction of «correctness», «appropriateness» or «decorum» as these concepts had been understood in the

(2) See page 323 of : *Romanticism* by Hugh Honour, 1979, Honour writes that : «The Romantic revolution... was like the battle which 'men fight and lose' in William Morris's *A Dream of John Ball* ; 'and the thing they fought for comes about in spite of their defeat, and when it turns out not to be what they meant, and other men have to fight for what they meant under another name'».

(3) For a great many of the ideas on Romanticism and Realism which have appeared in more recent texts, see : Léon Rosenthal *Du Romantisme au Réalisme, essai sur l'évaluation de la peinture en France de 1830 à 1848*, Paris, 1914. Note particularly Chapter III *Le Romantisme* and Chapter V *Le juste milieu*.

(4) See page 4 of *French Painting : Artists, Critics and Traditions from 1848 to 1870* by Joseph C. Sloane, Princeton, 1973 edition.

Fig. 1 - GÉRICAULT (cat. no. 65)

Classicism of the preceding period. In fact, one aspect of Romanticism could be defined as being, even more than the breaking down of centrality, «a progressive destruction of decorum - not... the absence of decorum, but the *process* of its destruction». (5) To define Romanticism presents a problem in that the Romantic artist was a spontaneous creator, very individualistic and thus opposed to being placed in any category. Baudelaire's definition may still be the best one : «Romanticism is neither exactly in the choice of subjects nor in exact truth but consists of a way of feeling». (6)

In spite of its often self-contradictory nature, Romanticism brought about many changes in the history of art. In beginning to break down the hierarchy of subject matter, Romanticism opened the way to the eventual emergence of landscape painting and the Barbizon School of Corot, Daubigny, Théodore Rousseau, Harpignies and others. Romanticism also represented a major step towards «pure painting» and the coming triumph of Manet. In addition, by beginning to eliminate the hierarchy of media, Romanticism re-awakened interest in the creative qualities of printmaking as well as in drawing and watercolor as independant and significant art forms. These latter developments were to be important for an artist such as Millet whose etchings and drawings were superior to his painting. Finally, through the liberating theories of Romanticism, artists were allowed to turn from history and religious painting to the painting of contemporary man himself, viewed both as isolated and as a fragment of a larger world. The long term effects of Romanticism have been profound. Just as the history of Europe was permanently altered by the French Revolution of 1789, the history of art was altered by Romanticism. In fact, «Romantic ideas about artistic creativity, originality, individuality, authenticity and integrity, the Romantic conception of the meaning and purpose of works of art and the role of the artist continue to dominate artistic thought...» (7)

*

*   *

The dates generally given to the Realist movement (already defined by Champfleury in his book *Réalisme* of 1847) cover a period of only seventeen years, from the exhibition of Courbet's *After Dinner in Ornans*, 1849 until 1866. In Realism, the emphasis was directed towards

(5) Page 38 of : *Romanticism and Realism* by Rosen and Zerner, New York, 1984.

(6) Baudelaire *Salon de 1846*, part II : «Le romantisme n'est précisément ni dans le choix des sujets ni dans la vérité exacte, mais dans la manière de sentir».

(7) Page 319 of : *Romanticism* by Hugh Honour, 1979.

quantitative rather than qualitative considerations. Man was seen to be of the same value as a still life or a landscape. The new ideal was to look with equal interest and objectivity at man and at the infinite variety of his surrounding world. In order to be objective, the artist (as well as the writer) was obliged to eliminate his subjective «Romantic» sentiments and to concentrate on outer Reality. The force of Realist art depended on the ability of the artist to create without expressing his feelings. A characteristic trait of Realism was its neutrality toward any subject matter. However, since the principles of Realism also included Romanticism's destruction of the hierarchy of subject matter, the «beautiful» and «grandiose» tended to be avoided. In Realism, the beautiful often was equated with the static and uninteresting while the ugly was equated with the dynamic and fascinating. It became important for the artist to truthfully depict an undistinguished or mediocre subject matter, without any attempt at idealization, picturesqueness or prettiness. This meant that the artist had to avoid those grandiose, rhetorical gestures on which visual art often had depended from the time of the Greeks until the middle of the nineteenth century. Once this move to the common was made and understood (in Courbet's *Burial at Ornans*, for example), the artist's strivings were freed from the subject matter and could concentrate on the style through which he was able to express a new beauty completely independent of the subject. The artist's task was not to make a given subject matter beautiful, but rather to create a beautiful picture.

In order to better understand Realism, four artists could be mentioned. These are Courbet, Millet, Daumier and Meryon. Of these, Gustave Courbet (1819-1877) was the one who, partially through his art and partially because of his strident, querelous personality, appeared to have made the most obvious attack on past tradition. In spite of the fact that his paintings were to a certain degree traditional and almost «classic» in the use of light, form and color, Courbet appeared revolutionary because of a number of his very large canvases depicting common and sometimes rather ugly people. These people were important personally to Courbet. He exalted their commoness and through them created a new beauty. For the general public and for most of the critics, however, these large paintings of common people were scandalous and represented an affront to the public's moral values as well as an affront to past traditions which had reserved such large paintings to the «historical» depictions of «kings and heroes, gods and saints».

Jean-François Millet (1814-1875), like Courbet, also rejected «historical» painting. However, instead of accepting only the surface appearance of things as had Courbet, Millet was taken by the inner qualities of simple people working in the fields. On the one hand, for Millet these peasants were as humbly attached to the ground as were cows and sheep. On the other hand, he depicted these same peasants as the noble representatives and as the sufferers of humanity in general. Millet, like Courbet, had rejected the heroes of the past. Different from Courbet, however, Millet had created a new kind of hero. Also different from Courbet, Millet had a more modern interest in the effects of light.

Honoré Daumier (1808-1879) was a painter, watercolorist, draughtsman and sculptor and also Europe's most talented lithographer in the middle of the nineteenth century. At a time when painting still ranked above other media, Daumier became known only as a lithographer. This considerably limited his influence in the development of Realism. Rather than depicting workers and peasants, as had Courbet and Millet, Daumier concentrated on the minds and spirits of the people in the streets of Paris. In his lithographs, Daumier had an uncanny power of raising the images of these common people to an astounding degree of universality.

The fourth artist whom we wish to cite relative to «Realism» is Charles Meryon (1821-1868). Meryon was one of the great artists of the 1850s and one of the most remarkable printmarkers of the nineteenth century. Solely an etcher, however, Meryon exerted limited influence (8) except in literary circles where he was recognized, particularly by Baudelaire : «Rarely have I seen the natural solemness of an immense city represented with more poetry». (9) Around 1850, when Baudelaire discovered the new theme of the beauty of the modern city,

(8)   That this prejudice against printmaking existed in the middle of the nineteenth century is not unusual. What is surprising though is that in the middle of the twentieth century, many books on nineteenth century French art hardly mention Meryon (for example, Meryon does not appear in the index of either Sloane's *French Painting 1848-1870* or in Rosen and Zerner's *Romanticism and Realism*). On the other hand, every book on the history of printmaking attaches the highest significance to this artist.

(9)   Charles Baudelaire *Salon de 1859*, part VIII : «J'ai rarement vu représentée avec plus de poésie la solennité naturelle d'une ville immense».

Fig. 2 - MANET   (cat. no. 87)

Meryon made this same discovery and expressed it in etching. More recently, referring to Meryon's *La Morgue* of 1854, Claude Roger-Marx speaks of the artist as «achieving almost the splendor and the silence of Rembrandt». (10) What distinguished Meryon's views of Paris was the primary role accorded to light, «a frank and solemn light which sculpted, chiselled and patined the bridges, facades, steeples and towers and which gave all these stones the brightness and sonority of bronze». (11) In depicting only the cityscape, Meryon, as had Courbet, Millet and Daumier, broke with the still lingering hierarchy of subject matter. Finally, in his use of light and in his seemingly cool detachment, Meryon pointed forward to the revolution of Manet and the advent of «pure painting».

*

*   *

The next movement in nineteenth century French art, Realism to «pure painting», also could be described as Realism to «modern art». Here we find a new emphasis on the physical appearance of the art material itself and a reconsideration of the artist's subjective reactions. No longer viewed essentially as a realist form, an object now was judged significant only in terms of the artist's response to that object. As «pure painting» developed, the artist's perspective was determined not so much by his thoughts but rather by the immediate, sensual impressions on his eyes. Among the initiators of this new movement, two artists could be considered. These artists are Corot and Manet.

«Modernism» in nineteenth century France could be said to have appeared first in the art of landscape. Here tradition was established less firmly than in figure-painting and a transformation of the artist's perception was more easily effected. Camille Corot (1796-1875) seemed at his best when he was working informally on landscape drawings and sketches. It was then that he achieved the greatest sense of liveliness and spontaneity. Corot, together with Daubigny, Théodore Rousseau and others of the Barbizon School shared a love of nature which they etched and sketched and painted in its fleeting and changing appearances rather than in its idealistic or imaginary forms. They contemplated nature freely, as individuals, giving way to a

(10) Page 90 of : *La Gravure Originale au XIXᵉ Siècle* by Claude Roger-Marx, Paris, 1962.

(11) Page 88 of Roger-Marx (opus cited). Compared to Daumier and Meryon, note similar ideas in photography. For example, Charles Negre, who lived near Daumier, and Disderi, apparently influenced by Courbet, photographed common people in Paris streets in the early 1850s, see page 29 and figures 6 and 7 of : Weston J. Naef *Regards sur la photographie en France au XIXe siècle*, Bibliothèque Nationale, Paris, 1980. Relative to Meryon, see photographs 4 (Du Camp), 23 (Le Gray), and 12 (Baldus).

direct, spontaneous response in their art. Through the Barbizon School, landscape came to be considered equal to other subject matters. This move away from the past also took place in figure painting. Here, however, it was a far more difficult development since the way man depicted man had a longer and more deep-seated tradition.

In Courbet's paintings, one senses the artist's involvement with his subject matter. On the contrary, in Meryon's etchings there is a certain detachment. In many of the works of Edouard Manet (1832-1883), this detachment becomes complete. Manet seems to use a given subject matter solely as an excuse for «pure painting». In his 1867 lithograph *Execution of Maximilian* (Fig. 2, cat. no. 87), for example, we see a line of men being executed by a firing squad. Manet's image indicates not a trace of emotion in what is a very emotional situation. The scene appears to have no significance in any moral or human sense. In view of the fact that almost every one of Manet's subject matters had been treated neutrally, the weight of artistic expression had been shifted completely to the temperament and style of the artist. This type of «pure painting» was most difficult for the 19th century critic to comprehend. For the basis of criticism also had to be shifted from the traditional way of seeing in preconceived categories to an immediate uncate- gorized attempt at understanding and appreciating the visions and feelings of the individual artist. The critic, for the first time, had to subordinate his ideas to those of each artist. The significance of what had been accomplished was summed up by Henri Matisse (12) : «Manet was the first painter who accomplished the translation of his sensations by liberating his instinct. He was the first to act through his reflexes and thus simplify the painter's profession, To do this, he had to eliminate everything which his education had given him, only keeping that which came from himself...».

In reviewing the progress of French nineteenth century art from Jacques-Louis David to Edouard Manet, we see many different steps from «traditional» to «modern art». The painting of David showed a hierarchy of subjects based on spiritual or moral worth. The importance of the subject matter determined artistic values. In the following period, in what has been called «objective naturalism», all visible objects, including man, took on an equal importance for the artist. Within this period, the «humanitarians» demanded still something more from the objects, namely that they be studied with the ideal of creating through them some sort of new morality. Turning away from «objective naturalism» and uninterested in «humanitarianism». Manet, in his «pure painting», concentrated only on the artist's subjective perception of the object. Reality thus had to be considered as an unchangeable element and the artist's temperament and creative ability alone embued the art work with its character and beauty. Edouard Manet did not suddenly invent this new artistic perception, he simply was the artist who in his work first defined it. In 1867, Emile Zola understood this : «... Our modern landscapists are far better than our history and genre painters because the landscapists have studied our countryside and were happy to interpret any corner of the forest which they saw. Edouard Manet applied the same method to each of his works. While the others beat their brains out (se creusent la tête) in order to invent a new *Death of Cesar* or a new *Socrates Drinking the Hemlock*, Manet simply places a few objects and people in his studio and begins to paint, analysing with care the nature of all that was in front of him». (13) In conclusion, if «progress» in modern art has been the liberation of the artistic mind from all preconceived ways of viewing and depicting an object and if «progress» has been to give primary importance to the individual artist's perceptions and feelings, then Manet could be considered as the first truly modern artist. (14).

*

* *

In his *Journal*, Eugène Delacroix described the role of the printmaker : «The language of the printmaker does not consist in only imitating the effects of painting which is still another language. For the printmaker has his own language which, even in a faithful translation of

(12) Page 122 of *Manet* by Michel Florisoone (quoted by Sloane on page 191).

(13) Emile Zola, *Une nouvelle manière en peinture : Edouard Manet*, from the article which appeared in the *Revue du XIXᵉ siècle* (directed by A. Houssaye), January 1st, 1867.

(14) See : Anne Coffin Hanson *Manet and the Modern Tradition*, New Haven and London, 1977 (note particularly section 8 of part II : *Modern History : Scenes of «La Vie Moderne»*).

another work, still allows him to shine forth his own personal expressiveness». As the nineteenth century advanced and the liberation of the artist from the hierarchy of media became ever more pronounced, draughtsmanship and particularly printmaking attained a renewed importance. Masters from Delacroix to Toulouse-Lautrec might be considered in attempting to clarify changing attitudes of artists, critics and the public towards different types of printmaking, towards original printmaking's relation to photography and to reproductive printmaking, and finally towards technical developments which gradually enlarged the artist's field of action.

A new invention at the beginning of the century, lithography flourished until the 1840s and then fell into disfavor. This was because the medium became principally a means for commercial diffusion and also because of the competition with photography which the public felt to be more effective as a «reproducer» than lithography. Etching, on the other hand, first was eclipsed by lithography and then also fell victim to photography. In the 1860s, there was a revival of interest in etching as an original art form. Animated by Bracquemond, Théophile Gautier and Baudelaire, in 1867 there was founded the *Société des Aquafortistes* (Society of Etchers), emphasizing the idea of originality in printmaking as a direct challenge to the threats of photography and reproductive print processes. This society, the first of its kind in France, included Bracquemond, Corot, Daubigny, Delacroix, Daumier, Millet, Fantin-Latour, Gavarni and Manet and, in 1865, Degas, Pissarro and Whistler. In spite of these developments in etching, around 1880 the medium again fell into disfavor at the same time that a new interest in lithography began and finally culminated in Toulouse-Lautrec, Bonnard, Vuillard and the blossoming of color lithography in the 1890s.

Examined more closely, all these developments were more intricate. For example, in the 1820s, when etching was not in vogue, Delacroix executed some of his most beautiful etchings, just as had Meryon in the 1850s when etching still was out of favor. In the 1860s and 1870s, when original lithography was not particularly appreciated, Daumier, Corot and Manet were creating some of their most beautiful lithographs. In 1880, when etching was out of fashion, Bresdin, Buhot, Degas and Pissarro executed some of their most exciting etchings. Finally, though lithography did not come again into full bloom until the 1890s, Redon, Fantin-Latour and Chéret were using the medium extensively throughout the 1880s and earlier.

Turning our attention to photography, it is interesting to note that Delacroix had been attracted to that medium because it realized one of Romanticism's greatest ideals : the immediate depiction of Reality without depending on any past tradition. Courbet's «objective naturalism» also wished to eliminate past traditions. The same principles here, however, in the hands of the mass of lesser artists around Courbet, resulted in imitation of reality rather than in creation. For these latter artists, photography became a distinct threat. By the 1850s, both lithography and etching had been overwhelmed by photography because the role of printmaking then was considered mainly to copy «original» works and to be a means of diffusion. Technical developments made photography a better medium for both of these tasks. In order to survive, printmakers gradually were forced to turn from what they saw to how they saw. In the 1860s, as has been mentioned, a new attitude towards printmaking developed in which the print came to be considered as an «original» art form without commercial objectives of either copying or imitation. Between this new attitude toward printmaking and the development of photomechanical processes, the role of reproductive printmaking gradually was eliminated. Thus, at the end of these struggles, there remained only original printmaking and photography which, no longer a threat to the printmaker, became one more way of enlarging the artist's means of expression.

Fig. 3 - COROT (cat. no. 23c)

Edgar Degas (1834-1917) executed paintings, pastels, watercolors, drawings, monotypes, lithographs, etchings, aquatints, and drypoints as well as sculpture and photography. While Manet, in his etchings and lithographs for example, made very few alterations in completed work, Degas made one change after another, resulting in a series of «states». His objective was to continually enrich or advance or experiment with his original concept. In this process, the final result was not necessarily better, but perhaps only different from an example of an earlier «state». These variations on a primary theme resulted in many unique, individual impressions, the exact opposite of the commercial concept of many multiples of an identical image. Like Buhot and Pissarro, Degas employed many techniques which are difficult to classify. For instance, he used an emery pencil or a carbon light rod to scratch fine dyrpoint lines on a plate, thus creating a grey, tonal effect. Degas also made over three hundred monotypes. (15) In these, with brushes, fingers or whatever came into his hands, he «painted» printer's ink onto a printing plate. He then was able to take one or two impressions from each plate. (16) Sometimes Degas transferred the ink of the monotype-plate onto a lithographic stone. Then, with a combination of drawing and scraping, he turned the original monotype into a lithograph. In the case of one work, for example *The Song of the Dog*, Degas started with a gouache whose photograph had been used in the preparation of a lithograph which in turn had itself begun as a monotype. (17) Degas often would add drawing and pastel to monotypes as well as to etchings and lithographs. He also used etchings, lithographs and monotypes as studies to be turned into pastels. Degas's later pastels of bathers and dancers sometimes look almost like sculptures, such was the sculptural nature of much of his art. In the 1880s and 1890s, Degas also executed some seventy-four sculptures in wax. These sculptures were used often as models for paintings, pastels, drawings, lithographs and other sculptures. (18) In constantly changing from one medium and one technique to another and in mixing media and techniques, Edgar Degas appears as the first modern artist completely free of the traditional hierarchy of media.

(15) See : *Degas Monotypes. Essay, catalogue and checklist* by Eugenia Parry Janis, Fogg Art Museum, 1968.

(16) Other artists who executed monotypes include : Appian, Buhot, Cassatt, Gauguin, Guérard and Pissarro. In this respect, see : *Nouvelles de l'estampe*, no. 19 of Jan-Feb, 1975 for two articles : Pages 16-23 *Les Monotypes de Camille Pissarro* by Barbara Shapiro and Michel Melot ; page 13 *L'estampe impressionniste et la réduction au dessin* by Michel Melot. See also pages 47-48 *Félix Buhot : Peintre-Graveur* by J.M. Fisher and C. Baxter, The Baltimore Museum of Art, 1983 for a discussion of Buhot's monotypes. See also in this last publication pages 43-45 for Buhot's use of photography.

(17) See : Douglas Druick and Peter Zegers, pages XXXVI-XXXVIII of : *Edgar Degas : The Painter as Printmaker* by Reed and Shapiro, Museum of Fine Arts, Boston, 1984.

(18) See : page 161 of : *Degas in the Art Institute of Chicago* by Richard R. Brettell and Suzanne Folds McCullagh, Chicago, 1984.

The 1890s in France saw a considerable increase of interest in printmaking. *L'Estampe Originale*, founded by Roger-Marx in 1889, published works by Rodin, Renoir, Gauguin, Redon and Toulouse-Lautrec and invited the participation of Bonnard, Vuillard and Roussel. Also in 1889 and publishing the same artists, Ambroise Vollard founded the *Peintres-Graveurs*. Vollard was one of the first to exhibit paintings and drawings together with prints. The interest in lithographs became particularly marked as they came to be considered as extensions of drawings. (19) Thus there developed the hand-signed print, the search for special printing papers and the cult of rareness for different proofs and states.

A great painter and superbly sensitive draughtsman, Henri de Toulouse-Lautrec (1864-1901) was captivated by lithography. Having grasped it possibilities from the very first, he devoted his enthusiasm and much of his time to this medium. (20) He not only mastered this art from aesthetic but also from technical aspects, including choices of paper and inks. He considered each impression and destroyed those which were not satisfactory. He also was known to have personally effaced his lithographic stones after the desired number of impressions had been pulled. (21) In the last ten years of his life, Toulouse-Lautrec, drawing directly on the lithographic stone and using an extraordinary visual memory, created a series of masterpieces. Through their simplification in outline and movement and with their singular arabesque quality, the lithographs, drawings and oil sketches of Toulouse-Lautrec in the 1890s made a definitive break with the impressionists who had followed Manet in the preceding decade. (22).

*

*   *

In the visual arts of nineteenth century France, we have seen a movement from what could be called «traditional art» to what might be called «modern art». The artists chosen to exemplify these developments included Géricault, Delacroix, Courbet, Millet, Daumier, Meryon, Corot, Manet, Degas and Toulouse-Lautrec. In this period, there were two fundamental changes in artistic attitudes. One, extending over the first seventy years of the century, concerned the breaking down of the hierarchy of subject matter. The second, extending from about 1840 to 1900, concerned the breaking down of the hierarchy of media with a new emphasis on drawing and printmaking as well as on the mixing and intermingling of media and techniques. Toward the end of the century, making use of these advances, a constellation of artistic geniuses including Degas, Toulouse-Lautrec and Cezanne created the foundation for the achievements of Picasso, Cubism and the following history of modern art.

R.STANLEY JOHNSON
March   1985

(19) See page 15 of : Michel Melot *L'estampe impressionniste et la réduction au dessin* in *Nouvelles de l'estampe*, No. 19, Jan.-Feb. 1975 : «Tout procédé qui assimile l'estampe au desin est recommandé : signature manuscrite, papiers recherchés, rarefaction des œuvres, différenciation des états et des épreuves.»

(20) See page 10 of : Claude-Roger Marx *La Gravure Originale au XIXe Siècle* : «In the sense that the poet, the true poet, finds a stimulation rather than a hindrance in rimes and metric rules, in the same way the printmaker receives from his medium a mysterious assistance and inspired solutions (to his artistic problems)».

(21) See pages 6 and 7 of : *Toulouse-Lautrec : Master of Graphic Art*, R.S. Johnson International, Fall, 1979.

(22) In our discussions, we have not included many of the major artists. Among these are : Pissarro, Renoir, Redon, Van Gogh, Seurat, Signac, Henri Rousseau, Gauguin, Rodin, Bonnard, Vuillard and others, particularly Monet and Cezanne.

CATALOGUE

1. **ADOLPHE APPIAN** (1818-1898)

Un Soir, Bords du Rhône à Rix (lst State), 1869.
Etching.
9 1/4 x 6 1/8 inches ; 157 x 236 mm.

Reference :
  Curtis & Prouté No. 27-I/III.

Notes :
  1. A very fine and rare proof before letters of the lst State (of three states). Curtis-Prouté call this state «rare» (R.).
  2. Appian was a rather isolated artist, having spent his whole life in the region of Lyons. Contemporary with Daubigny, this artist attempted to solve the same problems of changing luminosity at different times of the day which problems were to preoccupy the impressionist printmakers and particularly Pissarro. In 1912, Gustave Bourcard (in *La Cote des Estampes*) wrote that : «This absolutely remarkable artist-printmaker still remains unrecognized...». In 1974, Michel Melot in *L'Estampe Impressioniste* (Bibliothèque Nationale, Paris, 1974) writes that «without really having influenced Impressionism, Appian is a very representative artist concerned with the most avant-garde problems of his time with respect to the art of landscape».

2. **ADOLPHE APPIAN** (1818-1898)

Les Sources de l'Albarine (lst State), 1870.
Etching.
17 1/4 x 13 5/8 inches ; 438 x 345 mm.

Reference :
  Curtis-Prouté No. 29-I/V.

Notes :
  A very fine and rare proof before letters, pulled on thin Japan paper.
  Curtis-Prouté indicate that this lst State (of five states) is «très rare» (R.R.).

3. **ADOLPHE APPIAN** (1818-1898)

Un Jour d'Automne à Artemare (Ain), (lst State), 1871.
Etching.
6 1/8 x 9 1/2 inches ; 155 x 240 mm.

Reference :
  Curtis-Prouté No. 32-I/II.

Notes :
  A very fine and rare proof before letters, pulled on Chine fixé. Curtis-Prouté indicate that this lst State (of two states) is «rare» (R.).

4. **ADOLPHE APPIAN** (1818-1898)

Entrée du Village d'Artemare (Ain), (lst State), 1880.
Etching.
7 1/2 x 9 7/8 inches ; 190 x 250 mm.

Reference :
  Curtis-Prouté No. 58-I/III.

Notes :
  A very fine and rare proof before letters of the lst State (of three states).
  Curtis-Prouté indicate that this state is «rare» (R.).

1. APPIAN   Etching (Ist State), 1869

2. APPIAN   Etching (Ist State), 1870

5. **PAUL BERTHON** (1872-1909)

Notre-Dame de Paris, 1899.
Lithograph in colors : edition of 100.
22 1/4 x 16 1/2 inches.
Signed

References :
>   1. No. 34 and reproduced on page 118 of : *Berthon & Grasset* by Victor Arwas, New York, 1978.
>   2. Plate No. 79 and reproduced in color on page 71 of : *The Color Revolution : Color Lithography in France 1890-1900* by Phillip Dennis Cate and Sinclaire Hamilton Hitchings, Rutgers University Art Gallery, 1978.

Notes :
>   Berthon's talent for lithography had been enhanced through his training with his master Eugene Grasset as well as with Luc Olivier Merson who was a master technician but rarely did lithographs on his own account. Berthon also was helped by others at the various lithographic studios, particularly at the Imprimerie Chaix of Chéret fame. Among others, Berthon's lithographs include one of the most famous portraits of Sarah Bernhardt. Berthon's last known work was a poster for *Athalie*, a film starring Edouard de Max who had been the discovery of Sarah Bernhardt. This work was published posthumously in 1910, Berthon himself having died in 1909 at the age of thirty-seven.

6. **After LOUIS BOILLY** (1761-1845)

Revue du Quintidi, 1802.
Engraving in colors by Levachez and Duplessis-Bertaux.
17 x 11 3/8 inches ; 430 x 288 mm.

Reference :
>   Le Blanc 1.

Notes :
>   1. A superb impression of this rare portrait of Napoleon.
>   2. This engraving in colors was executed in July of 1802 (Thermidor An X) when the thirty-three year old Napoleon was designated «First Consul of France». At this time, the Accord of Amiens had just been concluded and a general peace had been re-established in Europe for the first time in ten years. To show its gratitude, the French people in August of 1802 was allowed to vote in a referendum asking : «Shall Napoleon Bonaparte be consul for life ?». An overwhelming majority of 3,500,000 to 10,000 accorded Napoleon a prolongation for life of this consulate. At the same time, Napoleon was given the right to designate his successor. Two years later in 1804, Napoleon was given the title of Emperor.

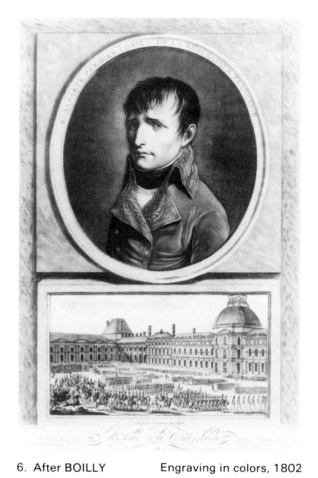

6. After BOILLY   Engraving in colors, 1802

7. **LOUIS-LÉOPOLDE BOILLY** (1761-1845)

Payez, passez or **L'Averse**, about 1805.
Pen, wash drawing and gouache.
12 5/8 x 15 3/4 inches ; 320 x 400 mm.
Below to the left, the stamp of the collection Georges Dormeuil (Lugt 1146a).

Exhibited :
1. *L.L. Boilly*, Galerie J. Seligman et Fils, Paris, June, 1930, no. 103 (exhibit presented by the *Société des Amis du Musée Carnavalet*, lent by Georges Dormeuil).
2. *Exposition d'Art Français*, London, 1932 under title of *Passez, payez, ou L'Averse*.
3. *Chefs-d'œuvre de l'Art Français*, no. 177 du catalogue.

Provenances :
1. Vente Goncourt, February 17, 1879 where bought by Monsieur Stettiner for 2.100 francs (information provided by Marianne Delafond, Curator at the Musée Marmottan - letter of February 12, 1985).
2. Georges Dormeuil.
3. No. 2 (reproduced in catalogue) of : *Dessins Anciens*, Ader-Picard-Tajan, Palais d'Orsay, Paris, June 13, 1978.

Notes :
1. This watercolor corresponds to the painting of the same subject, belonging to the Louvre in Paris (oil on canvas, 325 x 405 mm.). This painting was exhibited as No. 20 in : *Louis Boilly*, Musée Marmottan, Paris, May-June 1984. There also is a crayon drawing with white heightening (370 x 270 mm.) belonging to the Musée Marmottan (Inv. 384) and no. 76 in the 1984 Boilly exhibit at that museum. This latter drawing, showing only a sketch of the three figures to the right in the composition, also was in the 1930 Boilly exhibit *(Société des Amis du Musée Carnavalet)* where it was No. 115 of catalog. In the Musée Marmottan description of this other preparatory drawing (entitled *L'Averse* c. 1805), the catalog refers to this watercolor («dessin rehaussé d'aquarelle et d'encre de Chine... sous le titre *La Passerelle*», 320 x 400 mm.) as the watercolor in the Vente Goncourt of February 17, 1897.
2. Georges Dormeuil (1856-1939) appears to have been the owner of this work until his death in 1939. Dormeuil was one of the most reputed French collectors of recent times. He started his collection in about 1890 and actively collected until about 1922. His collection was magnificent and extended from the Haute Epoque to the early 19th century. He acquired drawings, paintings and other sorts of objects d'art. In 1934, Dormeuil made a major donation to the Louvre of Limoges enamels and other works from the 13th and 14th centuries. Also in 1934, Dormeuil presented the Musee Carnavalet in Paris with a group of works by Gabriel de Saint-Aubin. The strongest element of Dormeuil's collection consisted of paintings and particularly drawings of the 18th Century. The artists represented included Watteau, Fragonard, Gabriel de Saint-Aubin, Hubert Robert, Moreau le Jeune, Boucher, Greuze, Lavreince, Huet, Cochin, Portail, Lancret, Carmontelle, Leprince, Louis Moreau, Hoin, Mallet, Quentin de La Tour, Perronneau and Boilly.
3. At a time when Jacques-Louis David was turning major, political events into large «historical» paintings, Boilly described more modest occurences and genre scenes. Boilly diverged considerably from the norms of the academic painting of his time and showed a certain Realism which in subtle ways sometimes was quite avant-garde. This is one of the reasons for the recent renewal of interest in Boilly.

7. BOILLY   Drawing and gouache, about 1805

8. PIERRE BONNARD (1867-1947)

Boulevard, 1899.
Lithograph in colors : edition of 100.
6 7/8 x 17 1/8 inches ; 174 x 435 mm.

Reference :
Roger-Marx No. 61.

Notes :
1. A freshly colored impression. This work was plate 5 from : *Quelques Aspects de la Vie de Paris,* published by Ambroise Vollard in 1899.
2. There are several trial proofs of this work : before the color-change in the awning to upper-left ; before a figure appears towards the center between the 3rd and 4th trees ; and before spokes were added to wheel at far right. Claude Roger-Marx (page 116 of : *Bonnard Lithographe,* Monte-Carlo, 1952) indicates «two or three» such trial proofs. One of these was No. 2 and reproduced on page 9 of : *Important 19th and 20th Century Master Graphics,* R.S. Johnson, Chicago, Spring, 1983.
3. Colta Feller Ives (*The Great Wave : The Influence of Japanese Woodcuts on French Prints,* The Metropolitain Museum of Art, New York, 1974) notes that in Bonnard's own small collection of Ukiyo-e woodcuts, there were works by Kuniyoshi, Hiroshige and Kunisada. Ives (pages 60, 61, 62) feels that Bonnard's *Quelques aspects de la vie de Paris,* including this *Boulevard* of 1899 :

Perpetuates, the spirit of Hiroshige, whose myriad picture prints of Edo (Tokyo) and the sights along Japan's major roads (1830-1855) were popular with French collectors and well represented in Ukiyo-e exhibitions during the 1890's. (The catalogue of the exhibition at the Ecole des Beaux-Arts in 1890 lists sixty entries for albums and prints by Hiroshige. In 1893 S. Bing organized an exhibition of over three hundred prints by Hiroshige and Utamaro at the Durand-Ruel galleries). Both Hiroshige and Bonnard captured the animated life of the city in casual scenes of crowded boulevards, bridges and back streets... The spell of Hiroshige and Ukiyo-e landscape is cast upon Bonnard's entire suite of color prints.

Ives concludes (page 66) :

Japanese prints had broadened Bonnard's virwpoint and his palette. Their decisive role came in the early stages of his career when sympathetic with his talent and temperament, they provided the catalyst to complete his emancipation from time-worn western rules...

8b. PIERRE BONNARD (1867-1847)

Le Canotage, 1897.
Lithograph in colors : edition of 100.
10 1/4 x 18 1/2 inches ; 260 x 470 mm.

Reference :
Roger-Marx No. 44.

Notes :
A freshly colored impression. This work was for the 2nd Album of the *Peintres-Graveurs,* published by Ambroise Vollard.

8. BONNARD   Lithograph in colors, 1899

9. **FÉLIX BRACQUEMOND** (1833-1914)

Jeannot Lapin .
Etching.
9 3/4 x 13 3/8 inches ; 247 x 340 mm.
Signed, lower right.

Reference :
Not in Beraldi.

Provenance :
Formerly collection Alfred Beurdeley (Lugt 421)

10. **FÉLIX BRACQUEMOND** (1833-1914)

Les Hirondelles, about 1884.
Etching and drypoint.
13 1/6 x 11 inches ; 331 x 280 mm.
Signed lower right and with «B» stamp lower left.

Reference :
Beraldi No. 225.

Note :
This work, one of the artist's most important, appears to have been pulled in a total
edition of 100 impressions in this final state, each impression with the «B» stamp
lower left.

11. **FÉLIX BRACQUEMOND** (1833-1914)

Les Canards surpris (8th State) .
Etching.
14 3/4 x 10 5/8 inches ; 375 x 270 mm.
Signed and dedicated («a mon ami Maindron») to Maindron who did the first catalog on
Jules Cheret (*Les Affiches Illustrées 1886-1895* by Ernest Maindron).

Reference :
Beraldi No. 778-VIII/IX.

Note :
This appears to be the 8th State, with a tone laid on the left shoulder of the bather but
before the «B», lower left. On this cataloging see : page 47 of : *Felix Bracquemond and
the Etching Process,* College of Wooster Art Center Museum and John Carroll University Fine Arts Gallery, 1974.

9. BRACQUEMOND   Etching

10. BRACQUEMOND   Etching and drypoint,
about 1884

11. BRACQUEMOND   Etching

12. **RODOLPHE BRESDIN** (1825-1885)
Le Bon Samaritain (Ist Edition, 2nd State), 1861.
Lithograph.
22 1/4 x 17 3/8 inches ; 565 x 442 mm.

References :
1. Neumann No. 49.
2. Boon No. 76.
3. Van Gelder No. 100.

Notes :
1. This lithograph was first exhibited by Bresdin at the *Salon* of 1861 under the title of *Abd-el-Kader Helping a Christian*. The reference was to the Emir of Algeria, Abd-el-Kader (1808-1883) who had fought the French Army and who later was exiled to Damascus. In July, 1860, Abd-el-Kader personally saved the lives of thousands of Christians and Jews who would have been slaughtered by the Syrian Mussulmans. As a result of this charitable act, Abd-el-Kader became famous in France, inspiring many portraits, a play and various other artistic expressions, including this lithograph. Bresdin's lithograph portrays a symbol of Christian charity in the person of a non-Christian which subject Bresdin eventually felt encompassed the more general principle of a terrestrial paradise in which peace would reign.
2. This is one of the extremely rare earliest impressions of this lithograph, one of the masterpieces of 19th century printmaking. These earliest impressions are distinguished as being before the appearance of what looks like a small white bird to the lower left of the image. This «white bird» probably only was an accident to the lithographic stone, which accident took place just after the printing of a small number of trial proofs. In his article *Rodolphe Bresdin's Le Bon Samaritain* in the *Nouvelles de l'Estampe* (no. 70-71, Paris, July-October, 1983), David P. Becker of the Museum of Fine Arts of Boston indicates that there are only 21 known impressions of the *Bon Samaritain* before the appearance of the «white bird». These impressions are divided by Becker into two states depending on whether the monkey's leg, lower right in the image, is black or white, the impressions with the black monkey's leg being catalogued by Becker as being the 2nd State. Becker's list of the Ist State (before white bird and before the monkey's black leg) includes impressions at the Metropolitain Museum of Art in New York (on dark yellow chine collé) and at the Rijkmuseum in Amsterdam, the Museum Boymans-van-Beuningen in Rotterdam and the Clark Art Institute at Williamstown, Massachusetts (all these on white chine collé) and also at the Fogg Art Museum in Cambridge and two impressions at the Bibliothèque Nationale in Paris (these last three impressions on cream chine collé).
For the 2nd State, (all on cream chine collé), Becker notes the impression at the Gemeentemuseum in the Hague as well as the impression in the Paul Prouté Collection, Paris as well as the impression in the catalog. Finally, Becker notes, in private collections, four additional impressions which he has not been able to examine, as to whether they are of the Ist or 2nd State. Of Becker's 21 known impressions «before the white bird», 12 are in the Ist State, 5 (including this one) are in the 2nd State and 4 are as yet undetermined. Looking over these 21 impressions, 8 are in museums and 13 appear to still be in private collections.

12. BRESDIN   Lithograph (Ist Edition), 1861

13. FÉLIX BUHOT (1847-1898)

Une Matinée d'Hiver au Quai de l'Hôtel-Dieu (7th State), 1876.
Etching and drypoint.
9 3/8 x 12 5/8 inches ; 240 x 320 mm.

Reference :
    Bourcard-Goodfriend 123-VII/XV.

Notes :
    After its publication by Cadart in the 4th and 5th States, Buhot took this plate and re-worked it considerably. In his re-working, Buhot completely removed the signature as well as the sidewalk in this rare impression of the 7th State. The following 8th State is still without the etched signature, but the sidewalk is completely replaced and extended lower.

14. FÉLIX BUHOT (1847-1898)

Une Matinée d'Hiver au Quai de l'Hôtel-Dieu (11th State), 1876.
Etching, drypoint and aquatint.
9 3/8 x 12 5/8 inches ; 240 x 320 mm.

Reference :
    Bourcard-Goodfriend 123-XI/XV.

Notes :
    In the preceeding 10th State, this plate's lower margin is blank. In this very rare 11th State, a series of small sketches has been added to the blank margin below. Of the fifteen states of this work, these small sketches only appear in this rare 11th State : they are removed in the following 12th State and do not re-appear in the following states.

13. BUHOT   Etching and drypoint (7th State), 1876

14. BUHOT   Etching, drypoint and aquatint (11th State), 1876

15. **FÉLIX BUHOT** (1847-1898)

Convoi Funèbre au Boulevard de Clichy (3rd State), 1887.
Etching, drypoint and aquatint in colors. On heavy wove paper. With a pen and ink sketch of a head in upper-right margin.
11 5/8 x 15 3/8 inches ; 295 x 390 mm.
With Buhot's large red stamp (Lugt 977).

Reference :
Bourcard-Goodfriend No. 159-III/III.

Notes :
1. A brilliant impression of Buhot's masterpiece on color.
2. There exist a few rare proofs of this work with margins in black or gold. One of these (presently collection Mr. and Mrs. Reed O'Malley) was no. 43 and reproduced on page 51 of : *Felix Buhot*, R.S. Johnson, Chicago, February, 1983.

16. **FÉLIX BUHOT** (1847-1898)

Le Peintre de Marine (3rd State), about 1879.
Etching, drypoint and aquatint.
5 1/8 x 8 1/8 inches ; 130 x 207 mm.
With the artist's red stamp (Lugt 977).

Reference :
Bourcard-Goodfriend No. 146-III/IV.

17. **FÉLIX BUHOT** (1847-1898)

Le Peintre de Marine (3rd State), about 1879.
Etching, drypoint and aquatint.
5 1/8 x 8 1/8 inches ; 130 x 207 mm.
Signed lower right, indicated to far lower right : «Imprimé à 35 épreuves» (printed in 35 impressions) and with Buhot's red stamp (Lugt 977) far upper left.

Reference :
Bourcard-Goodfriend No. 146-III/IV.

Note :
For atmospheric effects, Buhot here employs a wove, tan paper. This results in an impression with a greater degree of dusk than the preceding impression from the same plate.

15. BUHOT   Etching, drypoint and aquatint in colors (3rd State), 1887

16. BUHOT   Etching, drypoint and aquatint (3rd State),
about 1879

18. PAUL CEZANNE (1839-1906)

Etude de Pins, executed about 1890-1895.
Pencil and watercolor.
21 5/8 x 17 inches ; 550 x 430 mm.

Provenances :
1. H. Silberberg, Breslan (sale, Paris, Galerie Georges Petit, June 9, 1932, no. 1).
2. Friedrich Wolff, Vienna.
3. Marlborough Fine Art, London.
4. Fritz Nathan, St. Gallen.
5. E.V. Thaw, New York.
6. Paul Rosenberg, New York.
7. Sotheby's, London, July lst, 1981, no. 314.

Exhibited :
1. London, Marlborough Fine Art, 1959, no. 11.
2. London, Marlborough Fine Art, 1960, no. 32.
3. Vienna, Belvedere *Paul Cezanne,* 1961, no. 71.
4. London, Lefevre Gallery : *Important XIX and XX Century Works on Paper,* 1977, no. 7 and reproduced on page 14 of catalog.

Literature :
1. Lionello Venturi, *Cezanne, son Art - son Oeuvre,* Paul Rosenberg, editeur, Paris, 1936, no. 982 (reproduced).
2. Peter Feist, *Paul Cezanne,* Leipzig, 1963, page 45, no. 10 (reproduced).

Notes :
On Cezanne's watercolors, Rainer-Maria Rilke wrote to a friend : «They are very beautiful. They reveal as much assurance as the paintings and are as light as the others are massive. Landscapes, brief pencil sketches upon which, here and there, as though to emphasize or confirm, falls casually a trace of color ; a succession of dashes, admirably arranged with a sureness of touch, like the echo of a melody».

18. CEZANNE   Pencil and watercolor, about 1890-1895

19. PAUL CEZANNE (1839-1906)

Les Baigneurs (small plate), 1896-1897
Lithograph in colors on chine volant.
9 1/4 x 11 1/2 inches ; 235 x 292 mm.

References :
1. Venturi No. 1156.
2. Druick No. III-4/4.

Notes :
1. A superb impression on chine volant with very fresh colors. This clearly is Druick's 4th State, published by Ambroise Vollard possibly about 1914 in about 100 impressions.
2. Cezanne executed three lithographs : the *Large Bathers,* the *Portrait of Cezanne* and the *Small Bathers.* There has been some confusion as to the order of execution as well as to the exact dating of these works. Douglas Druick, in his article *Cezanne's Lithographs* published as an essay in *Cezanne : The Late Work,* The Museum of Modern Art, New York, 1977, has divided the execution of these works in two parts ; first, the preparing of what were to be the black keystones for each of these lithographs ; second, the addition of color to two of these works and the publication of all three works. Druick points out (page 126 of the Museum of Modern Art catalog) that : «Unlike the keystone for the *Small Bathers,* those used in printing the *Large Bathers* and the *Portrait of Cezanne* were prepared by Clot (the printer) from drawings on lithographic transfer paper that he received from the artist.» Druick goes on to state (page 127) : «It is logical to assume that the black keystone for the *Small Bathers* was executed after he did the transfer drawings for the *Large Bathers* and the *Portrait of Cezanne...* Seemingly the artist would be most inclined to work directly on the stone only after he had become familiar with the medium... In the case of Cezanne, this hypothesis is supported by the fact that Clot apparently encouraged or persuaded artists who had worked on transfer paper to try drawing directly on the surface of the stone.» Druick sees, among these three lithographs : «... a basic difference of intention... the *Small Bathers* alone appears to have been executed with the intention of serving as the keystone in a color print. Its more abbreviated nature reflects the artist's awareness that he had to leave room for the addition of color.» Finally, Druick comments (page 128) that : «In the two transfer lithographs... the forms and the value relationships are more fully spelled out than in the *Small Bathers...* the color medium is used to reiterate the black-and-white statement... it is another reason for maintaining a chronology which places the *Portrait of Cezanne* and the *Large Bathers* before the *Small Bathers.*»
When it comes to the publication of Cezanne's three lithographs, Druick feels that the order of executions of the original works has been reversed. The *Small Bathers* (under the title of *Le Bain*) was the first to have been published by Ambroise Vollard, in his second album of 1897. On the other hand, Druick feels (page 128) that the preparation of the final maquettes for the *Portrait of Cezanne* (published in black-and-white only) and the *Large Bathers,* as well as the first color printing of the latter, was most likely done during the summer of 1898, when Cezanne was in Paris and Vollard was working with Clot on the preparation of the album for 1898.

20. PAUL CEZANNE (1839-1906)

Les Baigneurs (large plate), 1896-1897/1898
Lithograph in colors on laid paper with watermark MBM.
16 1/2 x 20 1/4 inches ; 420 x 515 mm.

References :
1. Venturi No. 1157.
2. Druick No. I-2/3.

Notes :
A very fine impression on laid paper with watermark MBM. The colors (ocher, blue, green, yellow, red and orange) and treatment corresponding to Druick's 2nd State. The 3rd State apparently does not contain the orange of this state and the colors are more translucent than these colors. Without the inscription below, this would correspond to a trial proof of this state, eventually pulled in about 100 impressions.

19. CEZANNE   Lithograph in colors, 1897

20. CEZANNE   Lithograph in colors, 1898

21. **THÉODORE CHASSERIAU** (1819-1856)

Venus Anadyomene (lst State), about 1841-1842.
Lithograph.
12 5/8 x 10 1/2 inches ; 320 x 266 mm.

References :
1. Bouvenne (1884) No. 25.
2. Beraldi (1886, Vol. IV) No. 25.
3. Bouvenne (1887) No. 10.
4. Chevillard (1893) No. 448.
5. Roger-Marx (1898) No. 25.
6. Caillac (in preparation) No. 2.
7. Sandoz (1974) No. 266.
8. Fisher (1979) No. 3.

Notes :
1. An extremely rare impression of the lst State (of two), still including the decorative border which was removed in the 2nd State. Jay M. Fisher on pages 146 and 147 of : *Théodore Chasseriau,* Baltimore Museum of Art, 1979, indicates only seven known impressions of this work in the lst State. Two of these had been in Paris (Paul Prouté catalogues *Colmar*, 1966, no. 159 and *Salimbeni*, 1973, no. 151). The other five lst States known to Fisher are in museums :
   Museum of Fine Arts, Boston.
   The Detroit Institute of Arts.
   The British Museum, London.
   Bibliothèque Nationale, Paris.
   National Gallery of Art, Washington, D.C.
2. Fisher (Baltimore, 1979) notes that this work was Chasseriau's first lithograph and is the most famous print in the artist's graphic œuvre. This lithograph was based on a painting *Venus marine*, dated 1838 and exhibited at the Salon of 1839. The painting is now in the Louvre (RF 2262) and is No. 44 in Marc Sandoz's *Théodore Chasseriau, 1819-1856 : Catalogue raisonné des peintures et estampes,* Paris, 1974.

21. CHASSERIAU   Lithograph (Ist State), about 1841-1842

22. JULES CHERET (1836-1933)

Théâtre des Fantoches (Ist State), 1900.
Lithograph-poster in colors.
40 x 32 1/4 inches ; 1195 x 820 mm.

Reference :
No. 471-I/II, reproduced in color as plate 24 and reproduced in color on the cover of :
The Posters of Jules Chéret by Lucy Broido, New York, 1980.

Notes :
1. This lithograph-poster is in the Ist State before letters. With letters, this poster advertised the Musée Grevin (wax museum) in Paris. This work was printed by the Imprimerie Chaix (ateliers Chéret) in Paris, rue Bergère near the *Folies-Bergère*.
2. In the 1880's, though being used extensively by Fantin-Latour and Odilon Redon, lithography had fallen out of favor. This situation changed abruptly in 1890. The element, on which the resurrection of lithography was based, was the addition of color.
The first artist to make use of color lithography was Géricault with his two-color lithograph *Retour de Russie* of 1818. Manet in 1874, with his *Polichinelle*, executed after a watercolor and with the use of seven lithographic stones, had established an example for other modern artists. The real catalyst however was Jules Cheret. For it was through their fascination with the color posters of Cheret, as well as with their discovery of Japanese prints, that painters found that a richly-colored palette could find its equivalent on a woodblock, a copper-plate or a lithographic stone. Color, which his predecessors had used rather indiscriminately in their lithographs, with Cheret found a new sense of liberty and movement. Cheret seemed instinctively to be able to combine his lithographic crayons in juxtaposing transparent and clear elements. Using the wildest fantasies, Cheret appeared to dash off his works with what seemed to be pure chance but with what really was the most exquisite sensitivity. With sharp, frenetic lines, with a hint of a blouse here, the point of a slipper there, Cheret defined the movements of a swiftly-moving dancer. Opposing full and empty spaces, creating large masses of reds, yellows, blues and oranges, contrasting modulations coming from rubbings and re-workings, juxtaposing one lithographic stone with another, Cheret's expertly created compositions developed their compositional solidity. As he worked, Cheret gradually eliminated all contours. Forms became for Cheret simply a pretext taken by the colors as an excuse to surge forward or flee into the background. Before Jules Cheret, color lithography had been an exacting and monotonous science. In the new development of color lithography, it was a combination of Cheret and the new influence of Japanese prints which really emancipated the eyes of the artists of the time. Following the direct inspiration of Cheret were the posters and lithographs of Toulouse-Lautrec. Also indebted to Cheret was a whole group of younger artists including Bonnard, Denis, Roussel, Signac and Vuillard who, around 1895, all also came to do color lithographs at the Clot studio. It was through the resurgence of interest in lithography, led by Cheret, that publications such as *L'Estampe Originale* of Roger-Marx and the *Peintres-Graveurs* of Ambroise Vollard became possible.

22. CHERET   Lithograph-poster in colors (lst State), 1900

23. CAMILLE JEAN-BAPTISTE COROT (1796-1875)

Paysage, about 1865-1870.
Charcoal drawing.
12 1/4 x 19 inches ; 311 x 483 mm.
Signed, lower right.

Provenance :
1. Tatischeff Collection, Paris.
2. Bellier Collection, Paris.

Note :
Dating from about 1865-1870, this is an outstanding drawing from Corot's later period. Nowhere is Corot more at ease than in his casual drawings such as this one. In these very personal and spontaneous sketches, we can see most clearly how Corot broke away from the concept of the traditional and classical landscape.

23b. CAMILLE JEAN-BAPTISTE COROT (1796-1875)

Le Fort détaché, 1874.
Autographie : edition of 100.
7 3/16 x 10 1/2 inches ; 182 x 265 mm.

Reference :
Delteil No. 32. As is normally the case, this impression is pulled on bulle volant paper.

23c. CAMILLE JEAN-BAPTISTE COROT (1796-1875)

La Lecture sous les Arbres, 1874.
Autographie : edition of 100.
10 1/4 x 7 1/4 inches ; 260 x 184 mm.

Reference :
Delteil No. 33. As is normally the case, this impression is pulled on bulle volant paper.

23. COROT   Charcoal drawing, about 1865-1870

24. **CAMILLE JEAN-BAPTISTE COROT** (1796-1875)

Souvenir d'Italie (Ist State), 1863.
Etching on Japan paper.
11 5/8 x 8 3/4 inches ; 294 x 222 mm.

Reference :
Delteil 5-I/IV.

Formerly collection :
Alphonse Hirsch (Lugt 563) : see also the biographic notes on Hirsch listed under Lugt 133). Alphonse Hirsch (1843-1884) was a Parisian painter and engraver whose portrait was etched by Degas in 1875 (Delteil 19). Hirsch also brought together a fine collection of etchings, particularly of Bracquemond and Meryon, Hirsch's collection was acquired in 1875 (the year of the death of Corot) by a Monsieur Carlin who thereupon sold the lot in a Sotheby auction on July 29-30, 1875. From said auction, Lugt describes the collection which included only one Corot : «Grand paysage en hauteur, sur Japon», which certainly is this one, and which was sold for three pounds and five schillings. This impression has Hirsch's initials, lower left, and Hirsch's stamp (Lugt 563), lower right.

Notes :
1. Michel Melot (*L'Oeuvre Gravé de Boudin, Corot, Daubigny, Dupré, Jongking, Millet, Théodore Rousseau*, Paris, 1978) has corrected the dating of this work by Beraldi (1865) and Delteil (1866) to 1863. Melot notes that this work was the first contribution by Corot to the *Société des Aquafortistes* where it was published on April 1, 1863.
2. This is one of the rare and very fresh proofs of this work «before letters». After the 2nd State with letters : «Cadart et Chevalier éditeurs, rue Richelieu 66» and «Imp. Delatre, rue Saint Jacques 303, Paris», there was a third printing with retouches in the background and other changes. In this latter printing, the corners of the plate were rounded. In this condition, Melot notes a printing in *L'Eau-forte depuis 10 ans,* with the address of Cadart. Finally, there was a tired and rather heavy-handed 4th State, printed «without letters».

25. **CAMILLE JEAN-BAPTISTE COROT** (1796-1875)

Le Clocher de St. Nicolas-les-Arras (2nd State), 1871.
Lithograph (autographe) : edition of 50.
10 5/8 x 8 1/2 inches ; 270 x 216 mm.

Reference :
Delteil 19-II/II.

Notes :
1. There were fifteen «autographes» executed by Corot. Of these, twelve (including this one) were published together in an edition of only fifty impressions. This edition was arranged by Alfred Robaut and was printed by the Imprimerie Lemercier in Paris.
2. The «drawing-like» quality of these «autographes» resulted from the methods employed by the artist. In the publication of 1872, this method was described as follows : these were «compositions drawn on autographic paper» by the artist, which compositions were then «transmitted directly onto the lithographic stone», by the Imprimerie Lemercier.

24. COROT   Etching (Ist State), 1866

25. COROT   Lithograph (autographe), 1871

26. **CHARLES-FRANÇOIS DAUBIGNY** (1817-1878)

Le Chemin de Halage.
Drawing in sanguine.
13 x 19 1/2 inches ; 330 x 494 mm.

Reference :
No. 176 and reproduced on page 214 of : *Daubigny : la vie et l'œuvre* by Madeleine Fidell-Beaufort and Janine Bailly-Herzberg, Editions Geoffroy-Dechaume, Paris, 1975.

Note :
The subject of the «Towing of Barges» was one that Daubigny had treated a number of times. In this respect, from the above cited book by Fidell-Beaufort and Bailly-Herzberg, see no. 206 *The Towing of the Barges* unsigned black chalk drawing belonging to the Cabinet des Dessins, Musée du Louvre, Paris.

27. **CHARLES-FRANÇOIS DAUBIGNY** (1817-1878)

Les petits oiseaux, 1850.
Etching.
5 7/8 x 4 inches ; 149 x 101 mm.

Reference :
Delteil No. 70.

28. **CHARLES-FRANÇOIS DAUBIGNY** (1817-1878)

Les Cerfs sous Bois, 1850.
Etching.
6 3/8 x 4 1/2 inches ; 162 x 113 mm.

Reference :
Delteil No. 82.

Note :
One of Daubigny's most famous and most reproduced graphic works.

26. DAUBIGNY   Drawing in sanguine

29. **CHARLES-FRANÇOIS DAUBIGNY** (1817-1878)

Le Grand Parc à Moutons (2nd State), 1860.
Etching.
7 1/4 x 13 1/2 inches ; 182 x 342 mm.

Reference :
Delteil No. 95-II/IV.

Notes :
    1. This rare 2nd State (of four states) was printed in only about 25 impressions in this form. This is one of Daubigny's major etchings. Daubigny also had executed a painting of this general composition. Exhibited in the *Salon de 1861*, this painting now is in the Mesdag Museum, The Hague, Holland.
    2. It should be noted that there exist false «before letters» impressions of this etching. These latter impressions were obtained either through covering up the lettered area or simply not inking the area in question. These latter impressions never include Daubigny's signature, while the true early impressions, such as this one, always include the etched signature.
    3. Melot (in : *L'Oeuvre Gravé de Boudin, Corot, Daubigny, Dupré, Jongkind, Millet, Théodore Rousseau,* Paris, 1978) notes that this etching originally had not been executed for Cadart's *Société des Aquafortistes* since the lst State dates from 1860 which was before Cadart had conceived of his project. Eventually Cadart did publish the print in the very first «cahier» of the *Société des Aquafortistes*.

30. **CHARLES-FRANÇOIS DAUBIGNY** (1817-1878)

Le Gué (2nd State), 1865.
Etching and drypoint with watermark : AQUA-FORTISTES.
9 7/8 x 13 3/8 inches ; 250 x 340 mm.

Reference :
Delteil No. 118-II/V.

Provenance :
    Ex-collection Jean-Felix Gautier (Lugt 1463a). Dr. Gautier (born in 1873) was a Colonel in the French Colonial Troops. He possessed a print collection with works dating principally from the 17th and 19th centuries (Callot, Van Dyck, Rembrandt, Nanteuil, Delacroix, Buhot, Daubigny and others).

Notes :
    1. This is one of Daubigny's major etchings. In this rare 2nd State (of five), Daubigny has terminated his print but the impression is before all letters except for the etched signature and the date. There apparently were only 25 such impressions and Delteil catalogs these impressions as «rare». In the following published 3rd State, the signature and the date have been removed and letters are added, indicating the printer to have been Delâtre and the publisher to have been Cadart & Luquet. In this form, *Le Gué* was included in the 1866 Album of the *Société des Aquafortistes*.
    2. Daubigny also executed a cliché-verre of this subject (Delteil no. 139) which Delteil dates 1862 and calls a «reminiscence» of the etching. Delteil thus appears to be mistaken in his dating of the cliché-verre since the etching which he dates 1865 would appear to follow rather than precede the cliché-verre.

31. **CHARLES-FRANÇOIS DAUBIGNY** (1817-1878)

Le Verger, 1868.
Etching.
7 3/8 x 4 3/4 inches ; 187 x 120 mm.

Reference :
Delteil No. 121.

29. DAUBIGNY   Etching (2nd State), 1860

30. DAUBIGNY   Etching and drypoint (2nd State), 1865

32. HONORÉ DAUMIER (1808-1879)

L'Accusation (Le Réquisitoire).
Pen and ink and wash.
7 5/8 x 10 11/16 inches ; 194 x 271 mm.
Signed, lower middle.

Provenances :
1. M. Villemot (1878)
2. Jos. Hessel, Paris.
3. Robert von Hirsch, Basel.

Exhibited :
1. Galerie Durand-Ruel, *Exposition des Peintures et Dessins d'H. Daumier,* no. 146, Paris, 1878.
2. Galerie Matthiesen, *Ausstellung Honoré Daumier ; Gemalde, Aquarelle und Zeichnungen,* no. 105, Berlin, 1926.
3. *Basler Privatbesitz,* no. 204, Basel.

Literature :
1. Arsene Alexandre, *Honoré Daumier - L'Homme et l'Oeuvre,* catalogued page 378, Paris, 1888.
2. K.E. Maison, *Honoré Daumier, Catalogue Raisonné of the Watercolors and Drawings,* Vol. II, no. 665, plate 254, Thames and Hudson, London, 1967.
3. No. 810 and reproduced in color on page 126, vol. IV of : *The Robert von Hirsch Collection,* London, 1978.

Notes :
A very similar drawing belongs to the collection of Mr. and Mrs. E.V. Thaw (see page 80 of : *Drawings From the Collection of Mr. and Mrs. E.V. Thaw* by Felice Stampfle and Cara Denison, New York, 1975). This latter drawing (Maison, Vol. II, no. 666, plate 254) has been compared to this one by Maison who points out that it is impossible to say which was the first version. Maison cites this pair of drawings as an example of Daumier's curious practice of repeating drawings in a «nervous pen-style that does not lend itself to line-by-line repetition».

32. DAUMIER   Pen and ink and watercolor

33. **HONORÉ DAUMIER** (1808-1879)

Le Ventre législatif, 1834.
Lithograph.
13 x 17 1/4 inches ; 325 x 435 mm.

Reference :
Delteil No. 131.

Notes :
1. A very rare proof, without trace of a center-fold and apparently before the edition published in January, 1834 by L'*Association mensuelle pour la Liberté de la Presse.*
2. In this work, Daumier was criticizing the French assembly which, together with the ruler of France, Louis-Philippe, seemed uncapable of bringing about any reforms.

34. **HONORÉ DAUMIER** (1808-1879)

Enfoncé Lafayette... Attrappe mon vieux, 1834.
Lithograph.
13 x 16 5/8 inches ; 325 x 420 mm.

Reference :
Delteil No. 134.

Notes :
1. A very rare proof, without trace of a center-fold and apparently before the edition published in May, 1834 by L'*Association mensuelle pour la Liberté de la Presse.*
2. In this work, Daumier makes fun of the false sorrows of the King, Louis-Philippe, on the occasion of the death of General Lafayette. Lafayette had become a popular hero through his part in the American Revolution. He also had been head of the French National Guard. Louis-Philippe did not like the popularity and prestige which Lafayette had achieved.

33. DAUMIER   Lithograph (proof), 1834

34. DAUMIER   Lithograph (proof), 1834

35. HONORÉ DAUMIER (1808-1879)

Il défend l'orphelin et la veuve, à moins... (2nd State), 1846.
Lithograph.
9 x 7 5/8 inches ; 229 x 194 mm.

References :
1. Plate 22 of the series : *Les Gens de Justice*.
2. Delteil 1358 II/II.

Notes :
An impression of the second state with letters, «sur blanc» on white wove paper. This is one of the deluxe edition (with no lettering on verso) before its inclusion in *le Charivari*, September 1, 1846.

36. HONORÉ DAUMIER (1808-1879)

Allongeons le pas... Voilà deux hommes (Ist State), 1848.
Lithograph.
9 3/4 x 8 1/8 inches ; 245 x 205 mm.

References :
1. Plate 4 of the series : *Les Alarmistes et les Alarmes.*
2. Delteil 1764 I/II.

Notes :
An impression «sur blanc» on white wove paper before letters above and below the image, and before letters on verso. The second state (with letters) was published in *le Charivari*, March 4, 1848. Delteil describes the first state as «Fort rare».

37. HONORÉ DAUMIER (1808-1879)

Tiens... Vous m'aviez dit... (2nd State), 1857.
Lithograph.
8 1/4 x 10 1/2 inches ; 208 x 267 mm.

References :
1. Plate 23 of the series : *Croquis Parisiens*
2. Delteil 2918 II/II.

Notes :
An impression of the second state with letters, «sur blanc» on white wove paper. This is one the deluxe edition impressions (with no lettering on verso) before its inclusion in *le Charivari*, January 21, 1857.

36. DAUMIER   Lithograph (Ist State), 1848

38. **EDGAR DEGAS** (1834-1917)

Danseuses dans la Coulisse (7th State), about 1879-1880.
Etching and drypoint.
5 1/2 x 4 1/8 inches ; 140 x 103 mm.

References :
1. Delteil No. 26-VII/VIII.
2. Adhemar No. 26-VII/VIII.
3. Reed/Shapiro No. 47-VII/VIII.

Notes :
1. In this 7th State of this extremely rare print, according to Delteil, the upper-most dancer (only whose hair was visible) of the 6th and preceeding states was replaced by another dancer clearly profiled to the left. In the following 8th State, there was new work by Degas on the curtain to the left, which curtain was enlarged and hides a part (her arm particularly) of the middle dancer whose profile turns to the right.
2. Delteil calls this state of this etching «fort rare» and only knew of the impression of the Alfred Beurdeley collection. Reed/Shapiro (Sue Welsh Reed and Barbara Stern Shapiro *Edgar Degas : The Painter as Printmaker*, Museum of Fine Arts, Boston, December, 1984) take note of the Beurdeley impression which appears to be the same one which now is at the Clark Institute. Reed/Shapiro also note three other known impressions of this work : this one (which had been no. 240, Kornfeld catalog, 1984 where it had been catalogued as an eighth state) ; the one at the Art Institute of Chicago (with atelier stamp) ; and finally an impression reworked with pastel (which reworking probably was done later according to Reed/Shapiro) which had been sold in New York on May 9, 1979 where it had been incorrectly catalogued as a fifth state.

38. DEGAS   Etching and drypoint (7th State), about 1879-1880

39. **EDGAR DEGAS** (1834-1917)

Femme nue debout, à sa toilette (4th State), about 1891-1892.
Lithograph.
13 1/4 x 9 5/8 inches ; 335 x 245 mm.
Signed, lower left.

References :
    1. Delteil No. 65-III/IV.
    2. Adhemar No. 63-III/IV.
    3. Reed/Shapiro No. 61-IV/VI.

Notes :
    1. Looking at the Delteil and Adhemar catalogs, we see a certain amount of confusion in the cataloguing of this rare work. In the first place, Delteil's illustration of his 3rd State has been incorrectly labeled by him as the «4th State». Adhemar adds to this confusion by first noting that Delteil had mislabeled his illustration, but then Adhemar mistakenly calls the illustration the «2nd State» when, as noted above, it was the 3rd State. On the basis of the Delteil and Adhemar catalogs, the correct cataloguing of this lithograph would appear to be as follows :

        Ist State : Before the long, falling hair of the woman. Adhemar knows of two such impressions : one of these is No. 162 of the 1918 Vente Degas, Bibliothèque de l'Université de Paris (collection Doucet).

        2nd State : With additional lines, modeling the body of the woman. Adhemar, following the indications of Kornfeld, indicates 4 know impressions which had been in the following collections : M. Guérin (sale of December 9, 1921), Beurdeley, Fenaille and A.H. Rouart.

        3rd State : With the falling hair of the woman, Adhemar indicates «a dozen impressions» including those in the Berlin Kupferstich-Kabinett, the Art Institute of Chicago, Bibliothèque Nationale de Paris, as well as this one.

        4th State : With the backing of the chair to middle-left taken away and other parts, notably the towel on the bed, lightened with «grattoir». Adhemar indicates «about ten proofs».

    2. Reed/Shapiro (Boston, 1984) have convincingly re-catalogued this work in six states. Particularly crucial for this impression are Reed/Shapiro's last three states :

        4th State : Backing of chair on middle-left and towel on bed are both treated strongly and darkly. This is the state of this lithograph.

        5th State : Backing of chair on middle-left and towel on bed are both considerably diminished and print very lightly.

        6th State : Backing of chair on middle-left completely eliminated while towel remains unchanged from preceding state.

39. DEGAS   Lithograph (4th State), about 1891-1892

40. EDGAR DEGAS (1834-1917)

Femme nue debout, à sa toilette (6th State), about 1891-1892.
Lithograph.
13 1/4 x 9 5/8 inches ; 335 x 245 mm.
Signed, lower left.

References :
    1. Delteil No. 65-IV/IV.
    2. Adhemar No. 63-IV/IV.
    3. Reed/Shapiro No. 61-VI/VI.

Exhibited :
    1. No. 18 and reproduced on page 4 of : *Important 19th & 20th Century Master Graphics,* R.S. Johnson, Chicago, 1976.
    2. No. S-23 in the Supplement to : *Degas in the Art Institute of Chicago* (Richard R. Brettell and Suzanne Folds McCullagh), Art Institute of Chicago, Fall, 1984.

Notes :
One of perhaps about ten proofs of the rare final state of this work. According to Reed/Shapiro (Boston, 1984), this final and 6th state of this work is to be distinguished by the fact that Degas eliminated completely the backing of chair on middle-left.

40. DEGAS   Lithograph (6th State), about 1891-1892

41. EDGAR DEGAS (1834-1917)

Femme après son Bain, about 1895.
Pastel with charcoal.
24 x 18 1/2 inches ; 610 x 470 mm.
With the stamped signature, recto (Lugt 658).
With the atelier stamp, verso (Lugt 657).

Provenance :

Paris, 1918 *Catalogue des Tableaux, Pastels et Dessins par Edgar Degas et provenant de son Atelier,* IIe Vente, December, 1918, No. 314, reproduced.

Exhibited :

No. S-26 in the Supplement to : *Degas in the Art Institute of Chicago* (Richard R. Brettell and Suzanne Folds McCullagh), Art Institute of Chicago, Fall, 1984.

Notes :

1. This study from about 1895 is one of many nudes which had been one of Degas's favorite themes since the 1800s. Degas has his own explanation for these nudes : «Here we have the 'bête humaine' which is concerned only with itself, a cat that licks itself. Until now, nudes were always shown in poses which were meant to please the public. My women, however, are simple and honorable people who only are concerned with their own physical well being. Here is still another one who is washing her feet : it is as though we were looking through a keyhole...» (P.A. Lemoisne *Degas et son œuvre*, Paris, 1947, page 118).

2. On page 126 of *Französiche Zeichnungen aus der Art Institute von Chicago*, Städelsches Kunstinstitut, Frankfurt, 1977, the catalogue entry by Dr. Harold Joachim and Suzanne Folds McCullagh describes a pastel of this period belonging to the Art Institute : «In our 'Après le bain, femme s'essuyant la jambe', Degas reaches a high degree of plasticity through his painterly handling of charcoal and pastel. This transforms linear qualities into plastic values, a research which Degas pursued at the same time in his sculpture... Degas's intense sense of animalistic sensuality, his capability to transform this sentiment into a effect of monumentality, his powerful draughtsmanship, all this make us understand why Picasso became such a great admirer of Degas».

41. DEGAS   Pastel with charcoal, about 1895

42. EDGAR DEGAS (1834-1917)

La Sortie du Bain : petite planche (Ist State), about 1891-1892.
Lithograph.
9 5/8 x 8 3/4 inches ; 245 x 221 mm.

References :
1. Delteil No. 63
2. Adhemar No. 67-I/II
3. Reed/Shapiro No. 65-I/II.

Exhibited :

No. 4 and reproduced on page 5 of : *19th and 20th Century Master Graphics*, R.S. Johnson, Chicago, 1974.

Notes :

1. Delteil already catalogued this extremely rare lithograph as «fort rare» and indicated only two impressions known to him (Bibliothèque de l'Université de Paris, Vente Degas).

2. Delteil indicates only this one state. However, there also exists the rare 2nd State, with the personnage in the background taken out of the composition. This 2nd State has been catalogued by both Adhemar and Reed/Shapiro.

3. As to the rareness of this work, Adhemar estimates that there were «a dozen» proofs. Of these, six had as provenance : Kornfeld und Klipstein in Bern. These latter proofs came from the collection of Exteens who had obtained them from his father-in-law Pellet (publisher of Toulouse-Lautrec's *Elles*), who had bought them from Degas. Known proofs of this work now are found at the Bibliothèque d'Art de l'Université de Paris, the Berlin Museum, the Rijksprentekabinet in Amsterdam, the Art Institute of Chicago, the Bibliothèque Nationale de Paris (apparently ex-collection Curtis), the Albertina Museum in Vienna and the Museum of Fine Arts in Boston. Finally, according to Adhemar, four proofs of this work are found in private collections. It would appear that this impression belongs to this latter group.

4. Reed/Shapiro note «some twenty impressions of the Ist State» including the one at the Albertina in Vienna which appears to be the only impression known to have the atelier stamp.

42. DEGAS   Lithograph (Ist State), about 1891-1892

43. **EDGAR DEGAS** (1834-1917)

Après le Bain, Femme s'essuyant la Jambe, about 1895.
Pastel.
24 5/8 x 20 1/4 inches ; 625 x 515 mm.
Red Degas atelier stamp, lower left (Lugt 657).

Literature :
    1. P.A. Lemoisne, *Degas et son Oeuvre,* Vol. III, No. 1436, reproduced.
    2. Paris, 1918, *Catalogue des Tableaux, Pastels et Dessins par Edgar Degas et provenant de son Atelier*, IIᵉ Vente, December, 1918, No. 187, reproduced.

Provenances :
    1. Ambroise Vollard, Paris.
    2. No. 40 and reproduced in *Vente de Collections provenant de Châteaux Etrangers*, Hôtel National, Lucerne, Switzerland, September, 1924.
    3. No. 33 and reproduced in color in Kornfeld Katalog No. 175, Bern, Switzerland, June 26, 1981.

Exhibited :
    No. S-28 in the Supplement to : *Degas in the Art Institute of Chicago* (Richard R. Brettell and Suzanne Folds McCullagh), Art Institute of Chicago, Fall, 1984.

43. DEGAS   Pastel, about 1895

44. EDGAR DEGAS (1834-1917)

Danseuse tenant son pied droit dans la main droite, 1890-1900
Bronze with back patina : the 4th cast of a total edition of 22 casts.
Height : 20 3/4 inches ; 528 mm.
Stamped with Degas's signature and CIRE PERDUE/A.A. HEBRARD and numbered 23/D.

Literature :
1. J. Rewald : *Degas, Works in Sculpture*, New York, 1957, p. 156, No. LXV, fig. 22.
2. F. Minerrino L'Opera completa di Degas, 1970, p. 142, no. S29.

Notes :
1. The «23» above refers to fact that this work was the 23rd of Degas's total production of 74 bronzes, while the «D» indicates that this was the 4th cast of the edition of 22 casts.
2. John Rewald *Degas, Works in Sculpture : a Complete Catalogue,* New York, 1944 (page 11) has presented a fine analysis of Degas's sculpture :

> While Degas had excelled at first with very smooth modelling, his technique toward the end became increasingly choppy and rough. His hands modelled the clay with more energy, less care, and their very feverishness seemed to be transmitted to the material. But this feverishness has nothing disordered about it, it corresponds to the almost youthful fire which so many great masters come to in their old age. The care for detail has disappeared ; both hand and eye go after what is essential with the raw strength which comes from knowledge and experience.
> We find this same strength in the summary outlines of his drawings and of his last pastels which are marked by a superb violence and colour. A grandiose vision is that of this old man who, in a profusion of forms, lines and colours, arrives at the pinnacle of a life filled with daring. The movements to which he had devoted such research he now represents in a style which is itself teeming with agitation - by vibrating lines and forms that seem alive. In his hands wax is no longer an inert material ; his fingers mould it almost with frenzy, constructing masses which no longer borrow from nature the smooth surface of human bodies, but express, right down to their rough texture, the pulsations of life and the breath of the creator.

44. DEGAS   Bronze, about 1890-1900

45. EDGAR DEGAS (1834-1917)

Danseuse regardant la plante de son pied droit, 1890-1900.
Bronze with black patina : the 8th cast of a total edition of 22 casts.
Height : 18 7/8 inches ; 480 mm.
Stamped with Degas's signature and CIRE/PERDUE/A.A. HEBRARD and numbered
59/H.

Literature :
1. J. Rewald : *Degas, Works in Sculpture,* New York, 1944, p. 27, no. LXI. See illustration : page 127.
2. J. Lassaigne and F. Minervino : *Tout l'Oeuvre peint de Degas*, Milano, 1970, p. 142. See illustration no. S34.
3. C.W. Millard : *The Sculpture of Edgar Degas,* Princeton, 1976 : pages 18-19.
4. Ian Dunlop : *Degas*, Ides et Calendes, Neuchatel, Switzerland, 1979 : No. 196 and illustrated on page 211.

Note :
The «59» above refers to fact that this work was the 59th of Degas' total production of 74 bronzes, while the «H» indicates that this was the 8th cast of the edition of 22 casts.

45. DEGAS   Bronze, about 1890-1900

46. EDGAR DEGAS (1834-1917)

Danseuse regardant la plante de son pied droit, about 1887-1890.
Bronze with brown patina : the 2nd cast of a total of 22 casts.
Height : 19 1/4 inches ; 490 mm.
Stamped with Degas's signature and CIRE PERDUE/A.A. HEBRARD and numbered 69/B.

Literature :
   1. John Rewald *Degas, Works in Sculpture, a Complete Catalogue,* 1944, no. XLIX, page 25, illustrated page 109.
   2. John Rewald *L'Oeuvre Sculpté de Degas,* 1957, No. IL, page 154, illustrated pages 59-60.

Provenance :
The estate of Harriet H. Jonas.

Exhibited :
   No. S-22, Fig. 76-1 and reproduced on page 161 in the Supplement to : *Degas in the Art Institute of Chicago* (Richard R. Brettell and Suzanne Folds McCullagh), Art Institute of Chicago, Fall, 1984.

Notes :
   The «69» above refers to fact that this work was the 69th of Degas's total production of 74 bronzes, while the «B» indicates that this was the 2nd cast of the edition of 22 casts.

46. DEGAS   Bronze, about 1887-1890

47. **EUGÈNE DELACROIX** (1798-1863)

Le Caid Mohammed-Ben-Abou : Chef Maure à Meknez (Ist State), 1833.
Etching.
4 1/4 x 6 3/4 inches ; 110 x 170 mm.

Reference :
   Delteil 22-I/II.

Note :
   A rare impression of the Ist State before letters.

48. **EUGÈNE DELACROIX** (1798-1863)

Le Caid Mohammed-Ben-Abou : Chef Maure à Meknez (2nd State), 1833.
Etching.
4 1/4 x 6 3/4 inches ; 110 x 170 mm.

Reference :
   Delteil 22-II/II.

Note :
   An impression of the 2nd State of this work with letters.

49. **EUGÈNE DELACROIX** (1798-1863)

Arabes d'Oran (5th State), 1833.
Etching.
5 5/8 x 7 1/2 inches ; 144 x 190 mm.

Reference :
   Delteil 20-V/VI.

Note :
   In this 5th State, the address of Delatre, present in the 4th State, is removed and replaced with : «Sarazin imp. Paris».

47. DELACROIX   Etching (lst State), 1833

48. DELACROIX   Etching (2nd State), 1833

50. **EUGÈNE DELACROIX** (1798-1863)

Rencontre de Cavaliers Maures, 1834.
Etching.
7 1/8 x 9 3/4 inches ; 181 x 249 mm.

Reference :
    Delteil 23.

Notes :
    1. Of this extremely rare etching, Delteil knew of only 6 impressions, three of which were in the *Vente Eugène Delacroix* and the others in the collections of F. Villot (sold in 1875), Edm. Hedouin (sold in 1889) and Champfleury (sold in 1891).
    2. It is to be noted that a lithographic copy of this work appeared in *Le Musée : Revue du Salon de 1834* by Alexandre Decamps. Delteil notes that Robaut mentioned a phototypographical reproduction of this work, published in *L'Art* of May 7, 1882. Finally Delteil also notes a copy of this etching in the form of a woodcut by C. Pingenet which apparently appeared in an issue of *Le Monde Illustré.*

51. **EUGÈNE DELACROIX** (1798-1863)

Nègre à cheval, 1823.
Lithograph.
6 1/2 x 8 1/4 inches ; 163 x 209 mm.

Reference :
    Delteil 39.

Notes :
    Delteil knew of only nine impressions of this rare work : in the Eugène Delacroix sale of 1864 (3 proofs), the Champfleury sale of 1891 (one proof), and the A. Robaut sale of 1907 (one proof) ; those in the Paris Bibliothèque Nationale and in the British Museum ; and finally those in the collections of A. Beurdeley and Moreau-Nélaton.

52. **EUGÈNE DELACROIX** (1798-1863)

Vercingétorix (2nd plate), 1829.
Lithograph.
9 7/8 x 7 1/8 inches ; 250 x 180 mm.

Reference :
    Delteil 90-II/II.

53. **EUGÈNE DELACROIX** (1798-1863)

Le jeune Clifford trouvant le corps de son Père, 1834.
Lithograph.
6 1/8 x 8 3/4 inches ; 155 x 222 mm.

Reference :
    Delteil 99-III/III.

Note :
    This is an interpretation by Delacroix from Shakespeare's *Henry VI.*

50. DELACROIX   Etching, 1834

51. DELACROIX   Lithograph, 1823

54. EUGÈNE DELACROIX (1798-1863)

Tigre Royal (undescribed State between II and III), 1829.
Lithograph.
12 7/8 x 18 1/4 inches ; 326 x 465 mm.

Exhibited :
No. 13 and reproduced on page 15 of : *Important 19th and 20th Century Master Graphics,* R.S. Johnson, Winter, 1977.

Reference :
Delteil No. 80-II or III/IV.

Notes :
1. A superb impression of one of the Masterpieces in the early history of lithography. This appears to be an undescribed state between Delteil's 2nd and 3rd States (of four States). Delteil's 2nd State is before all letters, while his 3rd State is with the title below *Tigre Royal* plus the address of the publisher. This impression has the title, but is still before the address.
2. In a letter of 1843 (quoted on page 53 of : *La Gravure Originale au XIXᵉ Siècle* by Claude Roger-Marx, Paris, 1962) to one of his students, Delacroix outlines his technique in lithography :

After you have drawn and filled in your lithographic stone, you must rub it until you have modelled the subject to your fantasy. Then, with a scraper, you must remove some of the blackness created, some more here and some less there, being careful not to go as deep as the grain of the stone itself. You must take some risks, but eventually you will master all this witchcraft (sorcellerie).

54. DELACROIX   Lithograph (undescribed State between II and III), 1829

55. **EUGÈNE DELACROIX** (1798-1863)

Muletiers de Tétuan (Ist State), 1833.
Lithograph on chine appliqué.
7 3/4 x 10 3/4 inches ; 196 x 274 mm.

Reference :
   Delteil No. 96-I/III.

Note :
   A strong, early impression of the very rare Ist State (of three States).

MULETIERS DE TETUAN.

55. DELACROIX   Lithograph (Ist State), 1833

56. GUSTAVE DORÉ (1832-1882)

But she to Almesbury fled all Night.
Long by glimmering Waste and Weald.
Pen and ink with gouache.
15 3/4 x 11 3/4 inches ; 400 x 300 mm.
Signed, lower right.

Notes :

   Doré would appear to be at his best in drawings such as this one. This particular work
   was executed as an illustration for Lord Tennyson's *Guinevere.* It later was engraved
   by J.H. Baker in 1887.

56. DORÉ   Pen and ink and gouache

57. **HENRI FANTIN-LATOUR** (1836-1904)

Portrait de Fantin à dix-sept ans (Ist State), 1892.
Lithograph on chine volant.
6 x 4 7/8 inches ; 151 x 124 mm.

Reference :
Hédiard No. 104-I/IV.

Notes :
1. This work was after a self-portrait of Fantin-Latour executed in 1853, when the artist was seventeen years old.
2. According to Hédiard, this rare Ist State was executed in two trial proofs plus an edition of 30. In the Ist State, there is a text below : «D'après le portrait que j'ai fait de moi à l'âge de dix-sept ans. H. Fantin». In the following state, this text was removed.

58. **HENRI FANTIN-LATOUR** (1836-1904)

Les Brodeuses (2e planche), 1895.
Lithograph.
7 7/8 x 12 5/8 inches ; 201 x 321 mm.

Reference :
Hédiard No. 123.

Notes :
1. Lithograph pulled in 275 impressions which appeared in L'Epreuve (August/September, 1895) under the title of Interieur.
2. Fantin-Latour executed three lithographs of this subject. The first of these : Les Brodeuses (1re planche) was after a drawing dated May, 1855. This work (Hédiard No. 4), according to Hédiard, was pulled in Lemercier's studio in only five or six proofs, after which the stone was destroyed. The second lithograph of this subject is the one in this catalog (Hédiard No. 123) and differs from Hédiard No. 4 in various ways including the fact that the face of the Brodeuse (Embroiderer) to the left no longer is visible. Also the right hand of the other Embroiderer rather than the left hand is working the cloth. And finally, the window handle is seen on the left-hand window in this second version. In the third lithograph of this subject Les Brodeuses (3e planche) ref. : Hédiard No. 143, Fantin-Latour employed a smaller format (165 x 211 mm.). This last work was pulled in seven or eight trial proofs, according to Hédiard, and then was published in the L'Estampe et L'Affiche edition of March 15, 1898.
3. The general composition of the above described three lithographs also was used by Fantin-Latour in the subject of Les Deux Sœurs. In this respect, we note the painting from 1859 in the St. Louis City Art Museum as well as the related etching (Hédiard etching no. 1, one of Fantin-Latour's two etchings) executed in 1862.

57. FANTIN-LATOUR   Lithograph
(Ist State), 1892

58. FANTIN-LATOUR   Lithograph, 1895

59. **HENRI FANTIN-LATOUR** (1836-1904)

Baigneuses (2ᵉ Grande Planche), 1881.
Lithograph on laid paper with watermark Name of Jesus.
13 7/8 x 14 3/8 inches ; 353 x 366 mm.
Signed in crayon, lower right.

Reference :
    Hédiard No. 38-II/II.

Notes :
    1. This is one of an edition of only twenty-five impressions printed by C. Lemercier, Paris.
    2. Hédiard (*Fantin-Latour : Catalogue de l'Oeuvre lithographique du Maître,* Paris, 1906), in his description of this work notes that a pastel of this subject had been exhibited in the Salon of 1893. Comparisons also could be made with Hédiard lithographs nos. 37, 128 and 138.

60. **HENRI FANTIN-LATOUR** (1836-1904)

La Source dans les bois (trial proof, third state), 1898.
Lithograph.
11 3/4 x 16 3/8 inches ; 300 x 415 mm.

Reference :
    Hédiard 139-III/III.

Notes :
    1. Along with Hédiard nos. 138, 140, 141, 142 and 146, this is one of the *Suite de Six Planches,* published by Ambroise Vollard in 1898.
    2. This impression is a trial proof on loose china paper, aside from the regular edition of 100 on chine appliqué.

59. FANTIN-LATOUR   Lithograph, 1881

60. FANTIN-LATOUR   Lithograph (trial proof, 3rd State), 1898

61. PAUL GAUGUIN (1848-1903)

Les Cigales et les Fourmis (Souvenir de la Martinique), 1889.
Zincograph on Canari paper : edition of 50.
8 1/4 x 10 1/4 inches ; 208 x 260 mm.

Reference :
Guérin No. 10.

Notes :
1. This work from the series of *Dix Zincographies*, is one of an edition of only 50 impressions on Canari paper, printed by Ancourt in 1889. There was a second edition of 50 more impressions on simili-Japan paper printed between 1893 and 1895.
2. The title of this work undoubtedly alludes to the well known fable by La Fontaine *La Cigale et la Fourmi.*

61. GAUGUIN

Zincograph, 1889

62. **PAUL GAUGUIN** (1848-1903)

Manao Tupapau, 1894.
Lithograph : edition of 100.
7 1/8 x 10 5/8 inches ; 181 x 272 mm.
Signed and numbered.

Reference :
Guérin No. 50.

Notes :
1. From the edition of 100 included in *L'Estampe Originale*, April-June, 1894 (with the blindstamp of the *L'Estampe Originale* in lower right margin).
2. This masterwork of 19th century lithography was executed by Gauguin in 1893-1894, between the artist's two trips to Tahiti. The subject of this lithograph was based on various drawings which Gauguin had brought back from Tahiti and had worked on in France at Pont-Aven from the Fall of 1893 onwards.

63. **PAUL GAUGUIN** (1848-1903)

Maruru, 1894.
Woodcut in colors.
8 1/8 x 14 inches ; 206 x 356 mm.

Reference :
Guérin No. 24.

Note :
One of 25 or 30 impressions pulled for Gauguin by the printer Louis Roy.

62. GAUGUIN   Lithograph, 1894

63. GAUGUIN   Woodcut in colors, 1894

64. **PAUL GAVARNI** (1804-1866)

Autoportrait avec cigarette (2nd State), 1842.
Lithograph.
10 1/4 x 7 1/4 inches ; 260 x 183 mm.

Reference :
Beraldi 141-II/V.

Note :
A very rare impression of the 2nd State (of five states) with the address of Bertauts to the left.

64. GAVARNI   Lithograph (2nd State), 1842

65. THÉODORE GÉRICAULT (1791-1824)

Retour de Russie (3rd State), 1818.
Lithograph in colors.
17 1/2 x 14 1/4 inches ; 444 x 362 mm.

References :
1. Delteil 13-I/II.
2. Géricault-Rouen 12.
3. Géricault 13-III/VI (see explanation below).

Formerly collections :
1. Amédée Faure (1801-1878). Faure was a student and eventually a professor at the Ecole des Beaux-Arts. He was a major collector of prints, particularly English works.
2. Private Collection, Nancy, France. Through direct descendance from Amédée Faure.
3. No. 225 and Tafel I in color of Kornfeld und Klipstein Katalog No. 183, June, 1983, Bern, Switzerland.

Notes :
1. This extremely rare work is the single most important example of early experimentation in color-lithography. Géricault executed this work only some twenty years after the invention of lithography by the German Alois Senefelder around 1798. The work was executed six years before the *Bulls of Bordeaux*, black and white lithographs of Goya. The date of 1818 for this lithograph was the same year that Senefelder first had published his book on lithography *Lehrbuch der Steindruckerei*.
2. In this lithograph, it had been Géricault's intention to honor the French soldiers who had fought in Russia in 1812. The achievements of these soldiers had been rather down-graded by the ruling Bourbons after 1814. Therefore, Géricault was expressing his sympathy for the Napolenoic past.
3. Delteil had indicated only two states of this work. Since then two catalogs have attempted to further clarify the more complex development of this lithograph. These were : Kate H. Spencer, *The Graphic Art of Géricault*, Yale University Art Gallery, New Haven. 1969, pp. 21 ; and R.M. Muthman in C.G. Boerner, *Neue Lagerliste 75 : Gedruckte Kunst 1460-1960*, 1981, No. 62. This new information on the various states of this work was summarized by E.W. Kornfeld *Moderne Kunst*, Bern, 1983, p. 46. In fact, it is clear that Delteil's original two states must be extended to six states, as follows :
   I. Before title below, with the address from Motte to left. Pulled with the black stone only.
   II. Before title below, with the address from Motte. Pulled with the black stone together with a brown tone-plate which allowed the cloud-areas to continue to the side directly.
   III. The same as II, but with the cloud-area limited.
   IV. The address of Motte to the left has been taken away. There are apparently two such known examples, in which the title and the new address have been written in by hand.
   V. With the printed title below : *Retour de Russie* ; and with the new address to the right :
   «Au Dépôt gal. de lithographie, Quai Voltaire no. 7». This 5th State was pulled with the black stone only.
   VI. The same as the 5th State, but pulled in two colors. The impression at the Art Institute of Chicago is of this final state.
The extremely fine and freshly-colored impression of our catalog corresponds to the above 3rd State : before the title, with Motte's address, but with the correction in the clouds. Such an impression is extraordinarily rare.
4. There is a drawing-study (in reverse) by Géricault for the figure on horseback in this lithograph : No. 113 and reproduced on page 229 of : *De Michel-Ange à Géricault : Dessins de la Donation Armand-Valton*, Ecole Nationale Supérieure des Beaux-Arts, Paris, May-July, 1981. In addition, there are three other known studies for this lithograph : one at the Art Institute of Chicago, another exhibited at the Los Angeles County Museum in 1972 (no. 59) and finally the drawing with brown ink and watercolor at the Musée des Beaux-Arts in Rouen. This latter study (No. 12ter and reproduced

Lithog.ᵉ de C.Motte Rüe des Marais f.ᵗ s.ᵗ germain.

65. GERICAULT   Lithograph in colors (3rd State), 1818

on page 37 of : *Géricault : Tout l'œuvre gravé et pièces en rapport*, Musée des Beaux-Arts, Rouen, November, 1981 - February, 1982) includes two other «returning» French soldiers besides the figure on foot and the figure on horseback which resemble fairly closely the two central figures in the final lithograph.

66. **THÉODORE GÉRICAULT** (1791-1824)

Marche dans le désert (2nd State), 1822.
Lithograph.
11 3/8 x 15 3/4 inches ; 290 x 401 mm.

References :
    1. Delteil 43-II/II.
    2. Géricault-Rouen 21.

Notes :
    1. As published in *Vie politique et militaire de Napoléon*, by A.-V. Arnault, French Academy, 1822-1826.
    2. Now quite rare, this was one of the major early works in the history of lithography.
    3. A drawing-study for this work is at the Ecole Nationale Supérieure des Beaux-Arts, Paris. This drawing was no. 21 bis and reproduced on page 48 of : *Géricault,* Musée des Beaux-Arts, Rouen, 1981.

67. **THÉODORE GÉRICAULT** (1791-1824)

Passage du Mont Saint-Bernard (4th State), 1822.
Lithograph.
14 1/16 x 16 3/8 inches ; 358 x 416 mm.

References :
    1. Delteil 44-IV/IV.
    2. Géricault-Rouen 22.

Notes :
    1. As published in *Vie politique et militaire de Napoléon* by A.V. Arnault, French Academy, 1822-26.
    2. Now quite rare, this was one of the major early works in the history of lithography.
    3. There is a drawing for this subject which belongs to the Ecole Nationale Supérieure des Beaux-Arts in Paris. This same drawing was no. 22 bis and reproduced on page 49 of : *Géricault : Tout l'œuvre gravé et pièces en rapport*, Musée des Beaux-Arts, Rouen, 1981.

67. GERICAULT   Lithograph (4th State), 1822

68. THÉODORE GÉRICAULT (1791-1824)

La jument et son poulain, frontispiece (3rd State), 1822.
Lithograph.
6 1/4 x 8 3/4 inches ; 153 x 218 mm.

References :
1. Delteil 46-III/V.
2. Géricault-Rouen 47.

Ex-collection :
Prof. Heinrich Schwarz (Lugt 1372).

Notes :
1. This is the frontispiece to the series of twelve lithographs by Géricault entitled : *Etudes de chevaux Lithographies,* published in 1822.
2. A rare impression of the 3rd State (of five) of this work.
3. This lithograph, with others of the same series, is particularly interesting as a «vignette». The idea of the «vignette» would appear to have been invented by Thomas Bewick at the end of the 19th Century (*A History of British Birds,* 1797 and Vol. II *Water Birds,* 1804). Up to this time, art appeared as «a view from a window» with clearly defined borders. In order to increase the unity between the texts and his illustrations, Bewick's borderless illustrations represented a revolutionary change. Géricault, after his trip with Nicolas Charlet to London in 1821, published his series of *Etudes de chevaux* in 1822. Bewick's revolutionary concept of the «vignette» is clear in this work by Géricault. Influenced by Géricault, Delacroix also used the «vignette» formula in lithographs such as *Baron Schwitters,* 1826 and *Cheval sauvage,* 1828.

69. THÉODORE GÉRICAULT (1791-1824)

Cheval de Mecklembourg (2nd State), 1822.
Lithograph.
7 3/8 x 9 1/4 inches ; 185 x 237 mm.

References :
1. Delteil 47-II/IV.
2. Géricault-Rouen 48.

Ex-collection :
Prof. Heinrich Schwarz (Lugt 1372).

Notes :
1. Plate 2 of : *Etudes Chevaux Lithographies.*
2. A rare impression of the 2nd State (of four) of this work.

70. THÉODORE GÉRICAULT (1791-1824)

Chevaux des Ardennes (2nd State), 1822.
Lithograph.
6 1/8 x 8 1/8 inches ; 158 x 208 mm.

References :
1. Delteil 51-II/IV.
2. Géricault-Rouen 52.

Ex-collection :
Prof. Heinrich Schwarz (Lugt 1372).

Notes :
1. Plate 6 of : *Etudes Chevaux Lithographies.*
2. A rare impression of the 2nd State (of four) of this work.

68. GERICAULT   Lithograph (3rd State), 1822

71. GERICAULT   Lithograph (2nd State), 1822

71. **THÉODORE GÉRICAULT** (1791-1824)

Cheval de la Plaine de Caen (2nd State), 1822.
Lithograph.
7 1/2 x 9 inches ; 192 x 227 mm.

References :
    1. Delteil 52-II/IV.
    2. Géricault-Rouen 53.

Ex-collection :
    Prof. Heinrich Schwarz (Lugt 1372).

Notes :
    1. Plate 7 of : *Etudes Chevaux.*
    2. A rare impression of the 2nd State (of four) of this work.

72. **THÉODORE GÉRICAULT** (1791-1824)

Les Boueux (3rd State), 1823.
Lithograph.
7 11/16 x 9 11/16 inches ; 195 x 246 mm.

References :
    1. Delteil 75-III/IV.
    2. Géricault-Rouen 89.

Notes :
    1. Plate 3 of the series : *Quatre sujets divers*, published in 1823 by Hulin.
    2. A rare impression of the 3rd State (of four) of this work.
    3. For this lithograph, there is a preliminary drawing-study at the Ecole Nationale Supérieure des Beaux-Arts, Paris. This drawing was no. 89 bis and reproduced on page 102 of *Géricault,* Musée des Beaux-Arts, Rouen, 1981.

73. **THÉODORE GÉRICAULT** (1791-1824)

Roulier montant une côte (2nd State), 1823.
Lithograph.
8 3/4 x 12 inches ; 222 x 305 mm.

References :
    1. Delteil 76-II/V.
    2. Géricault-Rouen 90.

Notes :
    1. A very rare (Delteil already catalogued this state as «assez rare») impression of Delteil's 2nd State (of five). In the following state, the address of Mme Hulin is removed.
    2. Delteil notes impressions of this state in the Bibliothèque de l'Ecole des Beaux-Arts in Paris, in the Musée Conde, at Chantilly and in the British Museum.

72. GERICAULT Lithograph (3rd State), 1823

73. GERICAULT Lithograph (2nd State), 1823

74. **HENRI-JOSEPH HARPIGNIES** (1819-1916)

Paysage au Bouquet d'Arbres - Crépuscule, 1850.
Etching.
Plate size : 7 1/8 x 10 inches ; 180 x 254 mm.
Image size : 5 3/16 x 8 1/4 inches : 132 x 210 mm.

References :
 1. Beraldi 24.
 2. Bibliothèque Nationale Inventory 10.

Note :
 This rare work, printed on chine appliqué, was printed in a very small edition.

75. **HENRI-JOSEPH HARPIGNIES** (1819-1916)

Scène de Campagne avec Moulin à Vent, 1879.
Watercolor.
21 x 14 3/4 inches ; 533 x 375 mm.
Signed and dated.

Notes :
 Harpignies was born in northern France at Valenciennes. In 1846, at the age of twenty-seven, he became a student of the landscapist and printmaker Jean Alexis Achard. Harpignies did landscapes in oil and watercolors in various parts of France. However, he was particularly attracted by the Barbizon School and especially by Corot. Harpignies spent a great deal of time at Barbizon and at Marlotte and drew and painted very often in the neighboring forests. The ease and openness of this work makes it one of the artist's most «impressionist» compositions.

76. **HENRI-JOSEPH HARPIGNIES** (1819-1916)

Vaches et Paysans dans un Grand Paysage, 1882.
Watercolor over traces of charcoal.
18 x 24 1/4 inches ; 455 x 615 mm.
Signed and dated.

Note :
 This large, open view of a forest scene is unusual for Harpignies both for the size of the format and also because of its grandiose conception.

75. HARPIGNIES   Watercolor, 1879

76. HARPIGNIES   Watercolor and charcoal, 1882

77. JEAN-AUGUSTE-DOMINIQUE INGRES (1780-1867)

Odalisque, 1825.
Lithograph.
5 1/4 x 8 1/4 inches ; 132 x 210 mm.

Reference :
Delteil No. 9.

Notes :
One of the most famous lithographs in the early history of lithography, this now very rare work was executed by Ingres after one of his own paintings of the same title, (*Odalisque*, 1813, Musée du Louvre, Paris). This *Odalisque* was included in an *Album lithographique* published by Delpech in 1826. With the exception of this work, all of Ingres's other graphic works were portraits. These consisted of only one etching and seven lithographs.

ODALISQUE.

77. INGRES   Lithograph, 1825

78. EUGÈNE LAMI (1800-1890)

The British Gallery at the Great Exhibition held in the Crystal Palace, London in 1851, with the Minton Stand on the right, 1851.
Pencil, Pen and brown ink, watercolor and bodycolor.
14 1/4 x 20 5/8 inches ; 362 x 524 mm.

Provenances :
1. Prince Anatole Demidoff ; for whom painted by Lami.
2. San Donato sale, July 2, 1875 : lot 320.
3. Estate of Stephen Richard Currier and Audrey Bruce Currier.

Literature :
1. P.A. Lemoisne *Eugène Lami*, 1912, pp. 123-124.
2. P.A. Lemoisne *L'Oeuvre d'Eugène Lami*, 1913, no. 860.

Notes :
1. Lami had been closely allied with Louis-Philippe and the French monarchists. When the reign of Louis-Philippe ended in 1848, the monarch fled to England where he died three years later. In 1848, Lami also fled to England. There he quickly became involved in the same fashionable circles he had known in France. Among Lami's friends from the past was Prince Demidoff who already had been depicted in Lami's 1840 group portrait (Lemoisne no. 739) executed in the Salon of Madame de Somailoff. P.A. Lemoisne (*Eugène Lami*, 1912, pages 122-123) notes that, after Lami arrived in England, Demidoff wrote about Lami to a mutual friend named Drum, suggesting that Drum «protect him and recommend him to your friends». After having seen the Russian section of the Great Exhibition held in the Crystal Palace in London in 1851, Demidoff decided to commission Lami to do a series of eight watercolors on the Great Exhibition. These watercolors, including this one, were then done in a series of eight duplicates which Demidoff wished to present to the Empress of Russia. According to Lemoisne, the first drawing for this series was executed in August 1851 and the series was completed around February, 1852.
2. Lami was one of the major early lithographers. His first lithograph, *Arlequin et Scapin discutant sur leur titre de famille* dated from 1817 when the artist was seventeen years old. In all, Lami executed some 344 lithographs over his lifetime. Lami also was a fine book illustrator. Among his illustrated works were *L'Hiver et l'Eté à Paris* by Jules Janin as well as *Les Oeuvres d'Alfred de Musset*. It was as a watercolorist, however, that Lami's talent achieved the most. Lami was one of the founders of the *Société des Aquarellistes français* with which group he exhibited his watercolors until the end of his long career.

78. LAMI   Pencil, pen and brown ink, watercolor and bodycolor, 1851

79. EUGÈNE LAMI (1800-1890)

Scène galante.
Watercolor.
8 3/8 x 12 3/8 inches ; 214 x 314 mm.
Signed with initials toward lower right.

Notes :

In this brilliantly colored and yet light and transparent «galant» dining scene, Lami shows his oft expressed admiration for the elegance of the past. He was particularly intrigued with Louis XIV and the life of Versailles. P.A. Lemoisne (pages 162 and 166-167 of : *Eugène Lami (1800-1890*, Paris, 1912) notes that Lami, both as an artist and a poet («en artiste et en poète»), loved Versailles. Lemoisne goes on to show that Lami had a particular ability, at Versailles, «to animate the old palace and give it back its soul» («le don d'animer le vieux palais, de lui redonner pour ainsi dire une âme»). In this respect, see pages 80-81 of *L'aquarelle en France au XIXe siècle,* 79e exposition du Cabinet des Dessins, Musée du Louvre, Paris, 1983.

80. MAXIMILIEN LUCE (1858-1941)

La Ferme (Le Mée), 1897.
Color lithograph on chine appliqué.
The «Bon à tirer» proof before the edition of 60.
10 5/8 x 14 1/8 inches ; 270 x 359 mm.
Signed & annotated : «Bon à tirer».

Notes :

Published by Gustave Pellet in a total edition of 60 (20 with a remarque, and 40 without the remarque), this is one of only seven color lithographs created by Luce. A proof marked «Bon à tirer» (literally «Good to pull») is the model for the edition, against which all other impressions are compared at the time of printing.

79. LAMI   Pencil, pen and brown ink, watercolor and bodycolor, 1851

81. EDOUARD MANET (1832-1883)

Les Petits Cavaliers (undescribed, intermediate state between the Ist and 2nd States), 1860.
Etching with drypoint on white Japan paper.
9 7/8 x 15 3/8 inches ; 251 x 391 mm.

References :
1. Guérin No. 8.
2. Wilson-Bareau (Ingelheim) No. 10.
3. Wilson-Bareau (Beres) No. 23.

Notes :
1. This is an unrecorded apparently unique intermediate state between the first and second states (of five states), with only some of the 2nd State's re-working and before much of the remodelling of the heads and bodies of the cavaliers. This fine impression is rich in burr and surface tone. The first state of this etching (British Museum) is strongly printed in blackish-brown ink. In this first state, Manet sketched only the bare outlines of the composition. As indicated by Guérin, the first state has a large defect in the upper sky. This defect is corrected in the second state and already is corrected in this intermediate state. Guérin indicates five known impressions of the first state, one of which (Museum of Fine Arts, Boston) is hand-colored and one of which belongs to the British Museum (donated by Campbell Dodgson in 1949). Of the second state, Guérin knows of only three impressions, one of which also is in the British Museum (also donated by Campbell Dodgson in 1949). In the British Museum's second state, printed on Japan appliqué, there is more shading work on the heads and bodies of the cavaliers in the central and righthand groups as wells as on the shadows cast on the ground. On the other hand, some of the shading on the backs of the figures at the left of the central group, visible in this intermediate state, has been burnished away in the second state. Finally, in the second state, there appears to be a diagonal burnishing mark to the left of the figure of the central group which mark is not yet present in this intermediate state.
One of the three 2nd State impressions, described by Guérin, now is in the collection of the Art Institute of Chicago. This impression, formerly in the collection of Guérin himself, is on Japan paper and was dedicated personally by Manet : «A mon ami Henri Hetch (sic for Hecht). Edouard Manet».
2. With an inscription on the backboard which reads : «Souvenir à Monsieur J. Jullien d'une petite eau-forte de Manet copie d'un tableau de Velasquez intitulé Seigneurs Espagnols - N'ayant d'autre mérite que d'être la seule épreuve produite. Bruxelles 26 juillet 78 Emile Kuesthor» (A souvenir for Monsieur J. Jullien of a little etching by Manet, a copy of a Velasquez painting called *Spanish Noblemen* - having no particular merit other than being a unique proof. Brussels, July 28, 1878. Emile Kuesthor).
3. Note that the cataloguing of this work in four states by Guérin has been superseded with Juliet Wilson Bareau's 1978 Paris catalogue chez Beres (see : cat. no. 23 and appendix). Wilson-Bareau has established five states. This does not effect the cataloguing of this work as a previously undescribed, intermediate proof between the first and second states (Reference : Juliet Wilson Bareau's letter of February 4th, 1985 to R. Stanley Johnson).

82. EDOUARD MANET (1832-1883)

Les Petits Cavaliers (3rd State), 1860.
Etching with drypoint on Halines paper.
9 3/4 x 15 1/4 inches ; 247 x 389 mm.

References :
1. Guérin No. 8-III/IV.
2. Wilson-Bareau (Ingelheim) No. 10.
3. Wilson-Bareau (Beres) No. 23-III/V.

Notes :
1. 3rd State (of four of Guérin ; of five of Wilson). From the first edition, published in 1862. In the Ist State of this work the composition is just sketched. The 2nd State is considerably re-worked. In the 3rd and published state, letters are added below : to the

81. MANET - Etching and drypoint (undescribed, intermediate state between the lst and 2nd states), 1860

82. MANET   Etching and drypoint (3rd State), 1860

left «Cadart et Chevalier éditeur ; in the center «Imp. Delatre Paris» ; and to the right «ed. Manet d'après Velasquez». In the following state, the texts are removed.

2. In 1851, the Louvre acquired a painting attributed to Velasquez (but now catalogued as «School of Velasquez») called *Reunion of Thirteen People* and now more well known as *Les Petits Cavaliers*. This painting attracted considerable attention at the time since there appeared to be a Velasquez self-portrait together with a portrait of Murillo to the extreme left of the painting. The painting must have been particularly interesting to Manet who liked to identify himself with Velasquez. As numerous art historians have noted, in Manet's famous depiction of «Modern Life» in the painting *Musique aux Tuilleries*, one sees the portraits of Baudelaire, Théophile Gautier, Offenbach and other artistic personalities : Wilson-Bareau (*Manet* chez Beres, Paris, 1978) notes that in his etching, Manet has placed his own self-portrait and the portrait of a painter-friend in a position parallel to the portraits of Velasquez and Murillo in Velasquez's (or «School of Velasquez») painting.

83. EDOUARD MANET (1832-1883)

Les Petits Cavaliers, 1860.
Etching with drypoint on laid Van Gelder paper.
9 3/4 x 15 1/4 inches ; 247 x 389 mm.

References :
1. Guérin No. 8-IV/IV.
2. Wilson-Bareau (Ingelheim) No. 10.
3. Wilson-Bareau (Beres) No. 23-IV/V.

Notes :
In this 4th State, the text below of the 1862 edition has been removed. This impression is from the Strolin edition of 100, published in 1905.

84. EDOUARD MANET (1832-1883)

Les Gitanos, 1862.
Etching.
12 1/4 x 9 1/8 inches ; 312 x 233 mm.
With blindstamp below : «Cadart et Chevaliers, 66 Rue de Richelieu».

References :
1. Guérin No. 21-II/II.
2. Wilson-Bareau (Ingelheim) No. 17.
3. Wilson-Bareau (Beres) No. 32-III/V.

Notes :
1. This is from an early part of the first edition, published by Cadart et Chevalier, Paris, 1862. In this first edition, there are letters below : to left «Manet sculpt» ; in center «Les Gitanos» ; to right «Imp. Delâtre, Rue des Feuillantines 4, Paris». In addition to the above, Guérin (*L'Oeuvre Gravé de Manet* by Marcel Guérin, 1944, Paris) notes a first early series of impressions, such as this one, with the blindstamp below of : «Cadart et Chevalier, 66 Rue Richelieu». In the later impressions (also of the 2nd State, first edition of 1862), the blindstamp below has been modified to read : «Cadart et Chevalier, 70 Rue de Richelieu».
2. Wilson-Bareau catalogues this work in five states (see : no. 17 in Ingelheim Manet catalogue) and makes a 2nd State out of a trial proof between Guérin's Ist and 2nd State.
3. This etching corresponds to a 1862 Manet painting which, for reasons unknown to us, Manet destroyed sometime after 1867. Manet kept some of the fragments of this painting. One of these corresponds to an etching after the figure in the back right of the etching : *The Water Drinker* (ref. : Guérin No. 22, Ingelheim No. 44 and Beres No. 33).

84. MANET   Etching, 1862

85. EDOUARD MANET (1832-1883)

La Marchande de Cierges, (Ist State), 1861.
Etching.
13 3/8 x 8 7/8 inches ; 339 x 227 mm.

References :
1. Guérin 19.
2. Harris 8.
3. Moreau-Nélaton 56.

Literature :
This impression (collection Loys Delteil) is reproduced facing page 36 in : *Manet : Aquafortiste et lithographe* by Léon Rosenthal, Paris, 1925.

Exhibited :
1. *Edouard Manet : L'Oeuvre gravé*, Ingelheim am Rhein, 1977 ; no. 7.
2. *Manet*, Huguette Bérès, Paris, 1978 : no. 31.

Formerly collections :
1. Gerstenberg.
2. Loys Delteil (with his stamp).

Notes :
1. As noted by Juliet Wilson-Bareau (author of the Manet catalogs of Ingelheim-am-Rhein, 1977 and of Bérès in Paris, 1978), there are only two known impressions of this work in the Ist State : this impression (which was No. 7 in the 1977 Ingelheim catalog) and the impression in the Detroit Institute of Arts (no. 70.5.578). There then is an apparently unique 2nd State impression reproduced in Marcel Guérin *L'Oeuvre Gravé de Manet*, Paris, 1944 (catalogued as formerly collections Edgar Degas, Philippe Burty and indicated by Guérin as now being Collection Le Garrec, Paris). In this 2nd State, there are numerous lines added, particularly in the frame at the top-back of the print. The 3rd State proof also is apparently unique. Wilson-Bareau indicates this 3rd State as also having been formerly collections Degas and Burty, but now in the Stockholm Nationalmuseum (no. 323, 1924). In the 3rd State, Manet added touches of aquatint to the front step, below the grill and under the kneeling desk and he also added cross-hatching to the face of the woman. In the Ingelheim catalog, Wilson-Bareau describes an apparently unique 4th State (Bibliothèque Nationale, Paris) with dark aquatint covering the whole plate. Wilson-Bareau finally notes what may be considered as a 5th State (New York Public Library, illustrated by Jean Harris, in her Manet book, as the «2nd State») in which still more aquatint has been added. From the 4th or 5th States, Wilson-Bareau notes a grand total of «5 or 6» known proofs. However, besides this Ist State impression, there is : the other Ist State at the Detroit Institute of Arts ; the unique known 2nd State (Collection Le Garrec) reproduced by Guerin ; the unique known 3rd State impression at the Stockholm Nationalmuseum ; the unique known 4th State impression at the Paris Bibliothèque Nationale ; and finally the unique known apparently 5th State impression at the New York Public Library. Thus, in all states, there are six known impressions of this rare work, four of which are in public collections.
2. In her letter of December 9th, 1984, referring to this proof, Juliet Wilson-Bareau states that : «*La Marchande de cierges* is a superb proof... Yes, it is the proof exhibited both at Ingelheim and chez Huguette Bérès the following year (1978), where we also had the 'new' 3rd State from Stockholm... The other Ist State is... in the Detroit Institute of Arts (ex-Ernest Rouart...). My notes on this proof give it on the same paper as yours (watermark HALLINES), with slightly dragged ink and printing indistinctly at lower right. Your proof prints extremely clearly... the impression is one of the most brilliant among all his artist's proofs...».
3. There is a question of Manet's intentions with respect to this etching. The etching of course did not appear in the *8 Gravures*, published in 1862. According to Wilson-Bareau, Manet did include the work in a proposed list of *14 Eaux-fortes*. Eventually Manet appears to have over-aquatinted this plate and then abandoned the idea of its inclusion even in the *14 Eaux-fortes*.
4. This is one of Manet's two «religious» etchings, the other being the *Christ aux Anges*. In both cases, the treatments of these works ran against the iconographical

85. MANET   Etching (Ist State), 1861

traditions then shaping the public mind. Wilson-Bareau (page 19 of Ingelheim catalog) points out however that there was a «traditional» aspect of these etchings and cites Théodore Duret who likes Manet's «Canaletto manner» and who likes the way Manet has «rediscovered Goya's picturesque animation». This «traditional» aspect of Manet was most special however in that the 18th century Venetians and Spanish painted in a baroque and «realist» manner opposed to the Raphaelesque tradition then being taught in the world of beaux-arts. To show to what extent this etching was avant-garde in 1860, in the Ingelheim catalog, Wilson-Bareau compares it to a very similar subject matter published in *L'Artiste* (Ed. Frere *La Porte du Paradis*, lithograph published in *L'Artiste*, T. XII, 1861). In this latter work, an almost identical scene, at almost the same time, is treated, in a more traditional, respectful manner, with a more conventional lighting effect. This same sense of modernity while painting a religious subject can be seen in the painting *Christ Mocked* (shown in the Salon of 1865) where Manet was not simply painting contemporary people in a realistic style but also had «caught poignantly the irresolutions of a century fighting equally hard against both past and future» (page 100 of : Anne Coffin Hanson *Manet and the Modern Tradition*, New Haven, 1979 edition).

86. **EDOUARD MANET** (1832-1883)

La Toilette (Ist State), 1861.
Etching.
11 1/4 x 8 7/8 inches ; 287 x 225 mm.

References :
1. Guérin 26.
2. Harris 20.
3. Moreau-Nélaton 9.

Literature :
This impression (collection Loys Delteil) is reproduced facing page 66 in : *Manet : Aquafortiste et lithographe* by Léon Rosenthal, Paris, 1925.

Exhibited :
1. *Edouard Manet : L'Oeuvre Gravé*, Ingelheim am Rhein, 1977 : no. 8.
2. *Manet*, Grand Palais, Paris, 1983 : no. 25, illustrated on page 93 (Ist State).
3. *Manet*, Metropolitan Museum of Art, New York : no. 25 and illustrated on page 93 (Ist State).

Formerly collection :
Loys Delteil.

Notes :
1. This is the same impression (from the Delteil collection) illustrated by Guérin which Guérin indicates is the unique impression in pure etching of the Ist State. Juliet Wilson-Bareau (Bérès, Paris, 1978) has discovered a second and rather differently inked impression of this Ist State which she now therefore catalogs as being in two known impressions.
2. There is a sanguine study for this work at the Courtauld Institute in London. This was no. 4 and reproduced in color in the Paris *Manet* exhibition chez Beres. In the Beres catalogue, Juliet Wilson-Bareau notes that : «This is a preparatory drawing for one of the most important etchings (*La Toilette*) of Manet at the beginning of his printmaking career. This composition... was transferred to the printing plate. Manet here uses a method which he was to use often. He traced the essential lines of the drawing with a pointed instrument which at times pierced the paper. Thus transferred to the surface of the printing plate, the composition was reversed in the proofs of the etching».
3. There is a still more complete drawing-study for this etching in the Helen Regenstein Collection at the Art Institute of Chicago (1967-30). This work is no. 73 and reproduced in color on page 149 of : *The Helen Regenstein Collection of European*

86. MANET

Etching (Ist State), 1861

Drawings, The Art Institute of Chicago, 1974 (catalogue by Harold X. Joachim). In his description of this drawing, Harold Joachim also refers to the etching :

> The drawings of Manet have needed a much longer time to find favor with collectors than his paintings and watercolors. The reason is that they are often diametrically opposed to the academic concept of what a drawing should be. If Rembrandt exasperated some of his contemporary critics by his lack of concern for the «correct» classical method, the sins of Manet provoked even greater ire. To be sure, Manet was not the practiced, untiring draughtsman Degas was : when he drew he did so entirely from the painter's point of view. No better example could be found than this sanguine drawing of a nude, *La Toilette*. It is a miraculous study of light playing on the soft texture of a female body, done with total disregard for anatomical correctness or the then prevailing concepts of beauty of form. In this respect, the drawing may well be compared with the nude studies of Rembrandt from the late 1650s. Although we have every reason to assume that the artist had a painting in mind, it did not materialize, and the work closest to our drawing is the etching *La Toilette*, published in 1862...

87. EDOUARD MANET (1832-1883)

L'Exécution de l'Empereur Maximilien, 1867.
Lithograph.
13 1/4 x 17 1/8 inches ; 335 x 435 mm.

References :
1. Guérin No. 73-II/II.
2. Wilson-Bareau (Ingelheim) No. 54.
3. Wilson-Bareau (Bérès) No. 77.

Notes :
1. A superb and richly inked impression on Chine collé, with the printed address of the publisher Lemercier below.
2. This famous work, a masterpiece from the whole graphic production of the 19th century, was not allowed to be published because of its political implications. It finally appeared in 1883, just after the death of Manet.
3. The subject of this lithograph, Maximilien Ferdinand was the «Ersherzog» from Austria and brother of the Kaiser Franz Joseph. In 1864, he accepted the Crown as Kaiser of Mexico. He lost the Crown in 1867 through the Mexican Revolution (and also because of the various French intrigues at that time). After being taken prisoner along with some of his faithful followers, Maximilien was executed in Queretaro on orders from Juarez.

87. MANET

Lithograph (2nd State), 1867

88. EDOUARD MANET (1832-1883)

Berthe Morisot (2nd State), 1872.
Lithograph on chine collé : edition of 100.
8 x 5 1/2 inches ; 204 x 140 mm.

References :
1. Guérin No. 77-II/II.
2. Wilson-Bareau (Ingelheim) No. 75 ; reproduced on cover of catalogue.
3. Wilson-Bareau (Bérès) No. 81.

Notes :
1. This is an impression from the now rare edition published by Lemercier in 1884. Guérin indicates that there are a number of 2nd State examples, such as this one, without visible letters («avec cache-lettre»).
2. This, one of Manet's major lithographs, is quite similar to Manet's painting of Berthe Morisot, dating from about 1872. Manet had been presented by Fantin-Latour to the Morisot sisters, both talented artists, in 1868. At this time, Manet wrote to Fantin-Latour (quoted by Juliette Wilson-Bareau in *Manet*, chez Bérès, 1978 : no. 81) :

> «... les demoiselles Morisot sont charmantes. C'est facheux qu'elles ne soient pas des hommes. Cependant, elles pourraient, comme femme, servir la cause de la peinture en épousant chacune un académicien et en mettant de la discorde dans le camp de ces gâteux». («The young Morisot sisters are charming. It's too bad that they are not men. On the other hand, as women, they could serve the cause of art if each one would marry an academic painter and then sow the seeds of discord in the camp of those unsavory characters»).

Berthe Morisot, at first Manet's model, gradually developed into one of the better impressionist painters. In 1874, she married Eugène Manet, the younger brother of Edouard Manet. It is quite possible that this lithograph was executed at the time of the marriage of Berthe Morisot and Eugène Manet. The lithograph was published by Lemercier just after Manet's death.

88. MANET   Lithograph (2nd State), 1872

89. ALBERT MARQUET (1875-1947)

Dessinateurs et Modèle, about 1898.
Charcoal drawing.
10 3/4 x 8 1/2 inches ; 273 x 216 mm.
Signed with initials, lower right.

Notes :

This drawing was executed at the time that Marquet and his comrade, Henri Matisse, were students together in Paris at the *Ecole des Arts Décoratifs*. Their professor was the artist Gustave Moreau who died in 1898. Later, in 1905, at the *Salon des Indépendants*, Marquet was to exhibit together with Braque, Derain, Dufy, Manguin, Matisse, Puy, Van Dongen and Vlaminck. This date marked the birth of Fauvism.

89. MARQUET   Charcoal drawing, about 1898

90. **CHARLES MERYON** (1821-1868)

La Galerie Notre-Dame (3rd State), 1853.
Etching.
11 1/4 x 7 inches ; 285 x 178 mm.

References :
Delteil-Wright No. 26-III/V.

Notes :
1. The quality of Meryon's etchings, even within a given state, have tremendous variance. This example, on China paper, is superb, with that great luminosity found in Meryon's most successful impressions.
2. The earliest known drawing for this work belongs to the Art Institute of Chicago (reproduced as cat. no. 26 in : *Charles Meryon : Prints & Drawings*, James D. Burke, Museums of Toledo, Yale and St. Louis, 1974-1975). The final drawing-study for this work is in the Paris Bibliothèque Nationale (A.C. 8516). James D. Burke (page 47 : see reference above), referring to the 3rd State of this etching (the state here exhibited) notes that :

«The third state was the first to be issued in any number, printed and published by the artist.

... Some extraordinary impressions were given a fine plate tone of sky, reflections on the colonettes and walks, highlights on the capitals in the dark corner, and the two heads of monsters above them.

Such attention to light does not exist in very even impressions of the later states, nor does the freshness of drypoint. The later states were carefully printed by Delâtre, with uniform attention to detail ; the subtlety Meryon desired is missing».

90. MERYON   Etching (3rd State), 1853

91. CHARLES MERYON (1821-1868)

Le Pont-au-Change (5th State), 1854.
Etching.

Reference :
Delteil No. 34-V/XI.

Notes :
1. A particularly fine and atmospheric impression of the 5th State (of Delteil's II states of this work). In the following 6th State, Meryon changed the open hearse on the bridge (to the left of the tower) to a covered wagon. In the 7th State of this work, Meryon completely eliminated the ballon *Speranza* in the sky, upper left.
2. There are some interesting pencil studies for this etching. One of these known to have been in the MacGeorge Collection, but present whereabouts unknown, apparently outlined the whole scene but without the man in the water in the foreground (see page 62 of : *Charles Meryon : Prints & Drawings,* catalogue by James D. Burke, museums of Toledo, Yale and St. Louis, September, 1974 - April, 1975). Another study is at the Art Institute of Chicago (No. 09.296). The complete and final study is in the Sterling and Francine Clark Art Institute in Williamstown, Massachusetts. In this latter pencil study, the balloon *Speranza* («Hope») above is seen clearly in contrast to the drama of the main struggling in the foreground waters below.

92. CHARLES MERYON (1821-1868)

L'Abside de Notre-Dame de Paris (4th State), 1854.
Etching on laid paper.
6 1/2 x 11 7/8 inches ; 165 x 295 mm.

Reference :
Delteil No. 38-IV/VIII.

Notes :
1. A superb, richly-inked, atmospheric impression of one of Meryon's most monumental etchings. Meryon impressions, such as this one, are becoming increasingly rare.
2. Meryon contemplated accompanying this etching with a poem but this was never published and this plate, with the poem, exists in just a few impressions. The poem reads :
> O thou who savored each Gothic morsel,
> Look upon Paris, proud edifice that our great and pious kings
> Wished to build for the Master
> In testimony of deep repentance.
> Although very large, it is alas, still too small, some say,
> To enclose the chosen of our least sinners.

3. There is a description of this etching by Philippe Burty (pages 83-84 i n : *L'Oeuvre de M. Charles Meryon II,* Gazette des Beaux-Arts, July, 1863). In this description, the «poet» in question obviously was Victor Hugo.
> The towers of the cathedral, seen from below the Pont de la Tournelle, dominate the apse and the buttresses. At left, the three arches of the Pont aux Choux, above which one sees the old structures of the hospital, and immediately at left the new construction.
> The view of Notre-Dame, previous to all help wich photography can give to draughtsmen today, is an imposing sight. The church of Notre-Dame seems also to have exerted a great attraction of the dreamy spirit of the artist. It has dictated to a poet one of the beautiful books of our generation ; it has inspired in Meryon his most beautiful plate.

91. MERYON

Etching (5th State), 1854

92. MERYON

Etching (4th State), 1854

93. CHARLES MERYON (1821-1868)

La Morgue (3rd State), 1854.
Etching.
8 3/8 x 7 1/2 inches ; 213 x 190 mm.

Reference :
Delteil No. 36-III/VII.

Provenance :
Collection Henri Thomas (Lugt 1378). Henri Thomas was one of the great print collectors in France in this century. The principal part of the Thomas collection was sold in Paris in 1952. This impression of *La Morgue* was no. 140 of the catalog in question : *Estampes des XIXe et XXe Siècles : Choix de Deux Cents Pièces de Qualité Exceptionnelle : COLLECTION H.T.* (Henri Thomas), Hôtel Drouot, Paris, June 18, 1952.

Notes :
1. A superb and extremely rare impression of the 3rd State (of seven states). In this state, the etching has been terminated but is before all letters.
2. According to James D. Burke (*Charles Meryon : Prints & Drawings*, Toledo, Yale and St. Louis, 1974-1975, page 70), there is only one known impression of the lst State of this work (Rosenwald Collection, National Gallery of Art, Washington D.C.). Burke indicates only two known impressions of the 2nd State (Cincinnati Art Museum and Bibliothèque Nationale in Paris). Burke only knows of eight impressions of the 3rd State (Cincinnati, Chicago, Detroit, London, New York Metropolitain Museum, New York Public Library, National Gallery in Washington D.C. and one in a private collection in New Jersey). This impression thus appears to be the ninth known impression of the 3rd State. Of these nine impressions, seven thus already are known to be in public collections.

93. MERYON

Etching (3rd State), 1854

94. CHARLES MERYON (1821-1868)

La Morgue (4th State), 1854.
Etching.
8 3/8 x 7 1/2 inches ; 213 x 190 mm.

Reference :
Delteil 36-IV/VII.

Formely collection :
Melvin and Mary Harrington (see their stamp on verso).

Notes :
1. An exceptionally fine and atmospheric impression of the 4th State (of seven states). In *Charles Meryon : Prints & Drawings* (museums of Toledo, Yale and St. Louis, September 1974 - April, 1975), James D. Burke notes that two extraordinary impressions of the 4th state in his exhibition «serve to indicate the great pains in etching and printing which Meryon took with this plate. He seems to have printed all the states up to the sixth himself, and many impressions bear evidence of this».
2. In *L'Oeuvre de M. Charles Meryon II* (which appeared in the *Gazette des Beaux-Arts* XIV of July, 1863), Philippe Burty describes this work : «In the eyes of some collectors, this etching is perhaps the most remarkable of all his works».
3. In the collection of the Art Institute of Chicago, there is another impression of this 4th State of a quality and particularly of a luminosity almost identical to this impression. The Art Institute's impression, from the Le Secq Collection, is accompanied by a card written by Loys Delteil, calling the impression «la plus belle épreuve que je connais de cet état» (the most beautiful proof of which I know of this state).

94. MERYON   Etching (4th State), 1854

95. JEAN-FRANÇOIS MILLET (1814-1875)

Une Bergère assise sur un Rocher, 1856.
Charcoal heightened with white chalk.
14 3/4 x 11 inches : 375 x 280 mm.
Signed, lower left.

Provenances :
1. H.A. Budgett.
2. Sale, London, Sotheby's, January 20, 1947, lot no. 167.
3. Lord Kenneth Clark, no. 24 of his collection, catalog. London, June-July, 1984.

Exhibited :
1. Probably, Paris, Ecole des Beaux-Arts, *J.F. Millet*, 1887, no. 166.
2. London, Leicester Galleries, *New Year Exhibition*, January, 1948, no. 8.
3. Aldeburgh, Moot Hall, Cardiff, National Museum of Wales and London, Arts Council Gallery, *Drawings by Jean-François Millet*, exhibition organized by the Arts Council, June-September, 1956, no. 30.
4. Hamburg, Cologne, Stuttgart, *Franzosische Zeichnungen*, 1958, no. 161.
5. London, Wildenstein & Co. *J.F. Millet*, November-December, 1969, no. 34.
6. Paris, Grand Palais, *Jean-François Millet*, October 1975 - January 1976, no. 81.
7. London, Hayward Gallery, *Jean-François Millet,* exhibition organized by the Arts Council, January-March, 1976, no. 56 (as Collection Lord Clark).

Notes :

This work, drawn in 1856, is similar in size and subject to two oil paintings by Millet of the same year. The American painter Edward Wheelwright acquired one of these. This was given to the Museum of Fine Arts in Boston, sold by that museum in 1939 and then given to the Cincinnati Art Museum in 1940. The second of these two paintings was executed by Millet for his friend Charles Tillot. At the time of the Wildenstein exhibition, this latter painting appeared to have been lost, but then reappeared later in a New York private collection namely that of Douglas Dillon. Subsequently, and very recently this painting was offered as a gift to the Metropolitan Museum in New York. In addition to the two paintings, there is a chalk drawing of this subject in the National Gallery of Scotland in Edinburgh. Finally, in 1862, Millet made his famous etching of this subject (Delteil No. 18) with the title of *La Grande Bergère*.

95. MILLET   Charcoal heightened with white chalk, 1856

96. JEAN-FRANÇOIS MILLET (1814-1875)

La Baratteuse (2nd State), 1855.
Etching.
7 x 4 3/4 inches ; 179 x 119 mm.

Reference :
Delteil 10-II/III.

Notes :
An extremely rare impression of the 2nd State (of three states), before the address of Delâtre but with the additional lines towards upper right and middle right, not found in the Ist State. Delâtre's address was added in the 3rd State. Delteil called this 2nd State «très rare».

97. JEAN-FRANÇOIS MILLET (1814-1875)

La Bouillie (2nd State), 1861.
Etching.
6 1/4 x 5 1/8 inches ; 158 x 130 mm.

Reference :
Delteil 17-II/V.

Notes :
1. An extremely rare impression of the 2nd State (of Delteil's five states) of this work, before the addition of the name of Millet but after the disappearance of the marginal sketches of the Ist State. Delteil knew of only one impression of this 2nd State in a Paris collection (J. Gerbeau).
2. Melot (*L'Oeuvre Gravé de Boudin, Corot, Daubigny, Dupré, Jongkind, Millet, Théodore Rousseau* by Michel Melot, Paris, 1978) notes 6 states of this work.
Ist State : before signature in plate and with marginal etched remarques. There are three such impressions according to Burty and four according to Lebrun. Of these one is at the Chicago Art Institute and another at Yale.
2nd State : still before signature in plate but without the marginal remarques. Of this state, there now are four known proofs : this one ; two at the Art Institute of Chicago and one at the New York Public Library.
3rd State is with etched signature ;
4th State with letters added below ;
5th State is a re-strike of the 4th State ;
6th State is still another and later re-strike of the 4th State.

96. MILLET   Etching (2nd State), 1855

97. MILLET   Etching (2nd State), 1861

98. JEAN-FRANÇOIS MILLET (1814-1875)

Les Glaneuses, 1855-1856.
Etching.
7 1/2 x 9 7/8 inches ; 190 x 252 mm.

Reference :
Delteil No. 12-II/II.

Notes :

1. Among works related to this famous etching, there is a black crayon drawing *Les Glaneuses*, 1852 from the Musée Grobet-Labadié in Marseille (no. 66 in : *Jean-François Millet*, Arts Council of Great Britain, 1976) as well as the oil painting *Les Glaneuses*, 1857 at the Musée du Louvre.

2. Millet's treatment of this subject showed a clear development. His first dealings with this theme just following the 1848 Revolution show simply happy harvest scenes in which the figures remain attached to the background. By the time of this etching (1855-56), Millet's work is strong in social content. Against the background of an apparently prosperous farm, we see the women in the foreground in the role of poor peasants only allowed to glean (hence the title *Les Glaneuses*) from the fields what has been overlooked by the harvesters. The attacks of conservative criticism against Millet's painting *Les Glaneuses* in the 1857 Salon had more to do with the painting's relatively revolutionary social message rather than with Millet's artistic qualities.

99. JEAN-FRANÇOIS MILLET (1814-1875)

Les bêcheurs (Ist State).
Etching.
9 5/16 x 13 1/4 inches ; 237 x 337 mm.

Reference :
Delteil No. 13-I/IV.

Notes :

1. This Ist State (of four states) is as described by Delteil : before the line around image and with the signature of Millet, upper right. In the following three states, the signature to upper right did not re-appear. Delteil describes this Ist State as «très rare» and cites only four such impressions known to him, namely those in the collections of A. Curtis, A. Rouart, Gerbeau as well as L. Delteil, Melot (*L'Oeuvre Gravé de Boudin, Corot, Daubigny, Dupré, Jongkind, Millet, Théodore Rousseau* by Michel Melot, Paris, 1978), on the other hand, notes that three impressions of this Ist State are now in museums : Bibliothèque Nationale in Paris ; Art Institute of Chicago ; and Yale University. It is probable that some or all of the impressions noted by Delteil to have been in private collections are the same ones now in the museums in question.

2. This particular impression was no. 18 and reproduced on page 25 of : *Important 19th & 20th Century Master Graphics,* R.S. Johnson, Spring, 1984.

3. See note 2 of cat. no. 98 of this catalog.

98. MILLET   Etching (2nd State), 1855-1856

99. MILLET   Etching (Ist State)

100. JEAN-FRANÇOIS MILLET (1814-1875)

Le Départ pour le Travail (Ist State), 1863.
Etching.
15 1/8 x 12 1/4 inches ; 385 x 310 mm.

Reference :
    Delteil 19-I/VI.

Notes :
    An extremely rare impression of the Ist State (of six states) of this work, before the
    addition of the etched name of Millet in the plate and before any address. The Ist State,
    which Delteil calls «fort rare», exists in perhaps fifteen or twenty impressions. Of these,
    ten had been given by Millet to various personal friends.
    These friends were :
        Jules Niel, Théodore Rousseau, Henri Tardiff, Charles Forget, Théodore Sensier,
        Michel Chassaing, Philippe Burty, Moureau, Charles Tiltot and Alfred Sessier.
    It had been Alfred Sensier who had the idea of putting together a sort of club to
    commission Millet to etch a plate. This club was to be called the *Société des Dix* (Club of
    Ten) and each of the ten members was to receive one personally dedicated impression
    of this etching. Of these ten dedicated impressions, two now belong to the Art Institute
    of Chicago, namely those dedicated to Théodore Rousseau (7ieme) and to Michel
    Chassaing (3ieme). Both of these impressions were dated by Millet as November 26,
    1863.
    It appears that Millet finished *Le Départ pour le Travail* on November 23, 1863, just
    three days before inscribing his dedications. The printer Delâtre brought these first
    proofs to Alfred Sensier on December 2, 1863. On December 15, 1863, Alfred Sensier
    wrote (quoted by Melot on page 288 of : *L'Oeuvre Gravé de Boudin, Corot, Daubigny,
    Dupré, Jongkind, Millet, Théodore Rousseau,* Paris, 1978) : «I will put the first ten
    impressions of your etching in the hands of Monsieur Rousseau Père so that you will be
    able to dedicate each one...». In fact, as indicated by the dates on the Art Institute's
    impressions, by this date already had inscribed his dedications.
    On December 28, 1863, Sensier writes (quoted by Melot on page 289, see above) :
    «Burty fells as you that the 2nd State is too heavy and oily. He complains strongly
    concerning these impressions (of the 2nd State) or rather of the new mania of Delâtre
    to push his proofs towards blacks and heaviness. He will come with me to Delâtre's
    when the 3rd and 4th States will be printed...». In conclusion, sometime between
    November 29 and December 28, 1863, Delâtre already had printed what we now (and
    also back in 1863) catalog as this etching's 2nd State with Millet's etched name added
    to the plate.

101. JEAN-FRANÇOIS MILLET (1814-1875)

Le Départ pour le Travail (4th State), 1863.
Etching.
15 1/8 x 12 3/16 inches ; 385 x 310 mm.

Reference :
    Delteil 19-IV/VII.

Notes :
    A very fine and rare impression of the 4th State (of seven) of this work, before there
    were added three points etched between the two lines, lower right. In the following 5th
    State, the three points are added as well as two other lines, forming a complete frame
    around the points. Delteil notes that the 6th and 7th States were pulled posthumously.
    In the 6th State, the lines indicating the clouds above are extended to within 30 mm. of
    the right border, whereas in all previous states these lines of clouds were 65 mm. from
    the same border.

100. MILLET   Etching (lst State), 1863

102. CAMILLE PISSARRO (1831-1903)

Femme vidant une Brouette (2nd State), 1880.
Etching.
12 5/8 x 9 inches ; 319 x 230 mm.

Reference :
Delteil 31-II/XI.

Notes :
1. Delteil notes that the 3rd State (illustrated in Delteil's catalog) has about 20 lines added in back of the wheel-barrow, has various stones added to the right of the tree and has various lines added to the dress of the peasant woman. This 2nd State impression is before all these additional lines. In view of the fact that Delteil is not able to describe a «lst State» of this work and states that he has never seen à «lst State», it could be possible that the «2nd State» actually is the «lst State» of this etching.
2. Delteil notes that this 2nd State was pulled in «4 or 5 proofs».

102. PISSARRO   Etching (2nd State), 1880

103. CAMILLE PISSARRO (1831-1903)

Femme vidant une Brouette (4th State), 1880.
Etching.
12 5/8 x 9 inches : 319 x 230 mm.
Annotated by the artist : «6ᵉ état no. 1», «femme vidant une brouette» and «manière grise».

Reference :
Delteil No. 31-IV/XI.

Notes :
This impression, following Delteil's descriptions, could be either Delteil's 4th or 5th State in spite of being annotated by Pissarro as the 6th State («6ᵉ état no. 1»). However, in comparing this impression with the 5th State in the Library of Congress (information provided by Barbara Shapiro of the Museum of Fine Arts, Boston), this would appear to be clearly the 4th State. Delteil notes that the 4th State was pulled in two impressions (1 and 2) of which this appears to be the first.

103. PISSARRO   Etching (4th State), 1880

104. **CAMILLE PISSARRO** (1831-1903)

Paysage sous Bois, à l'Hermitage (Pontoise), 1879.
Etching : edition of 50.
8 5/8 x 10 1/8 inches ; 219 x 269 mm.
Signed.

Reference :
    Delteil 16-V/V.

Notes :
    This etching had been destined to be included in an art publication : *Le Jour et la Nuit*.
    Other artists to have been included in the same project were Degas, Bracquemond and
    Mary Cassatt. This publication project was never realised.

105. **CAMILLE PISSARRO** (1831-1903)

Baigneuses à l'ombre des berges boisées (trial proof, 2nd State), 1894.
Zinc lithograph on chine appliqué : trial proof.
6 x 8 1/2 inches : 152 x 215 mm.
Signed.

Reference :
    Delteil 142-II/II.

Notes :
    1. Delteil states that there are 14 numbered impressions of the Ist State. This is one of
    a few trial proofs of the 2nd State before the edition of 100 published in *l'Estampe
    Originale*, March, 1895. After this edition there are a further 12 impressions numbered
    101 to 112.
    2. Pissarro previously had contributed an etching (Delteil 70) to *L'Estampe Originale* in
    the album of spring 1894. In a letter of March 3, 1893, Marty, the editor, had first asked
    Pissarro for a print. This particular lithograph already was being made in January,
    1894 (see : Marty's letters of January 21 and 28, 1894). Therefore, in spite of its
    publication in 1895, we have given this work the date of 1894. On this, see page 53 of :
    Frances Carey and Antony Griffiths *From Manet to Toulouse-Lautrec : French Litho-
    graphs 1860-1900*. The British Museum, London, 1978.

104. PISSARRO   Etching, 1879

105. PISSARRO   Lithograph (trial proof, 2nd State), 1895

106. CAMILLE PISSARRO (1831-1903)

Récolte de pommes de terre (6th State), 1886.
Etching.
11 x 8 5/8 inches ; 280 x 220 mm.
Signed : «C. Pissarro», annotated : «No. 3 - 6e état», and titled : «Récolte de Pommes de terre».

Reference :
   Delteil 63-VI/VII.

Notes :
   Delteil notes that the lst State of this work was pulled in 2 proofs, the 2nd State in 1 proof, the 3rd State in 2 proofs, the 4th State in 1 proof, the 5th State in 1 proof, this 6th State in 3 proofs and the final state in «a dozen proofs». Delteil's various states correspond to Pissarro's own annotations.

107. CAMILLE PISSARRO (1831-1903)

Repos du Dimanche dans le Bois (3rd State), 1891.
Etching and drypoint.
7 x 11 3/8 inches ; 176 x 289 mm.
Signed : «C. Pissarro», annotated : «2e état - no. 4» and titled : «Repos dans le bois (Z)».

Reference :
   Delteil 99-III/III.

Notes :
   1. The «(Z)» in Pissarro's annotation refers to the fact that this work was pulled with a zinc plate.
   2. Delteil notes a lst State of this work, sketched only in drypoint and pulled in two proofs. Delteil then notes a 2nd State with numerous additions but still lacking the «general effect» of the final state. According to Delteil, there was only one proof of this 2nd State, proof annotated by the artist : «1er épr. d'état entre le 1er et le 2e état... Repos dans le bois» (lst trial proof between the lst and 2nd State... Resting in the woods). In Delteil's 3rd State (which Pissarro calls his 2nd State), the whole plate has been re-worked. Delteil notes that this 3rd State was pulled in 14 impressions, each numbered, signed and annotated as the «2nd State» by the artist. This impression is the no. 4 of the edition of 14. There also was a posthumous edition of 18 proofs which were numbered and stamped.
   3. It is to be noted that in April of this same year (1891), Pissarro (a Danish citizen born on the island of St. Thomas) and the American Mary Cassatt, because they were «foreigners», had been denied the right to participate in the 1891 exhibit of the *Société des Peintres-Graveurs Français* which took place at the Galerie Durand-Ruel in Paris. This was particularly upsetting to Pissarro in that the first «official» recognition which he had received had been because of his participation in the 1890 exhibition of the same group at which exhibition the Superintendent of Fine Art, Burty, had acquired two of his etchings. In view of the above it was a great satisfaction for Pissarro and Cassatt that Durand-Ruel accorded them together a «two-man» exhibition of their graphic works which exhibit took place in the Galerie Durand-Ruel at exactly the same time as the exhibit of the *Société des Peintres-Graveurs Français*. At this time, Pissarro wrote to his son Lucien :
      «Nous ouvrons samedi en même temps que les patriotes qui, entre nous soit dit, vont être furieux d'apprendre qu'à côté il y aura une exposition de choses rares, exquises». (We are opening on Saturday at the same time as the patriots who, let it be said between the two of us, are going to be furious to find out that right alongside of their own exhibition, there will be another exhibition of rare and exquisite things). Quoted in chapter XX of *Pissarro* by R.E. Shikes and P. Harper.

106. PISSARRO   Etching (6th State), 1886

107. PISSARRO   Etching and drypoint (3rd State), 1891

108. **CAMILLE PISSARRO** (1831-1903)

Baigneuse près d'un bois (4th State), about 1896.
Zinc lithograph on chine appliqué.
One of 4 proofs in this state.
8 1/8 x 4 15/16 inches ; 207 x 125 mm.
Signed, titled and numbered «Ep defi no 2».

Reference :
Delteil 158 IV/IV.

Notes :
Delteil states that there are 4 proofs of the final state, of which three are signed and numbered. There is also a posthumous edition of 18 which are stamped and numbered.

109. **CAMILLE PISSARRO** (1831-1903)

Grand'Mère (La femme de l'artiste), about 1895.
Zinc lithograph : edition of 10.
9 3/8 x 5 inches : 238 x 127 mm.
Signed & numbered «no. 9».

Reference :
Delteil 143.

Notes :
Delteil states an edition of 10 numbered impressions, for the most part signed. There were also 6 additional impressions printed posthumously in 1923, not mentioned by Delteil.

108. PISSARRO   Lithograph (4th State), about 1896

109. PISSARRO   Lithograph, about 1895

110. CAMILLE PISSARRO (1831-1903)

Eglise et Ferme d'Eragny (6th State), 1890.
Etching in black, red, blue and yellow.
6 3/8 x 9 7/8 inches ; 162 x 251 mm.
With Pissarro's stamped initials (Lugt 613e) and inscribed «Ep. d'essai».

Reference :
Delteil No. 96-VI/VI.

Notes :
1. Delteil indicates six states of this work, pulled in black and white in a total of 11 proofs. In addition, Delteil refers to a series of proofs of this work pulled in colors through the use of four separate plates. These latter proofs mix various color combinations. Delteil indicates three such proofs in the lst State, four proofs in the 2nd State, two proofs of the 3rd State, two proofs of the 4th State and four proofs of the 5th State, a total of fifteen impressions. Of these, the Art Institute of Chicago possesses an impression, retouched in chalk (annotated «No. 2, 5e état La Ferme à Eragny») which served as model for color proofs printed in the 6th State.
2. Michel Melot (*The Graphic Works of the Impressionists,* New York, 1972 : Pissarro no. 91) notes that seven black-white impressions of this work were pulled in 1923. Finally, there were eleven proofs plus perhaps a few trial proofs pulled by Porcabœuf in 1930 after the plates were cancelled. One of these is this impression and another belongs to the Art Institute of Chicago. In both of these impressions, there is the Pissarro studio stamp (Lugt 613e) and both are annotated in the same hand «ép. d'essai».

111. CAMILLE PISSARRO (1831-1903)

La Charrue, 1901.
Lithograph in colors.
8 7/8 x 6 1/8 inches ; 225 x 155 mm.
With signature in stone.

Reference :
Delteil No. 194-II/II.

Notes :
1. A particularly freshly-colored impression, used as a frontispiece for a booklet by Kropotkin in the series *Les Temps Nouveaux.*
2. Delteil indicates a date of 1901 for this work while Michel Melot (*The Graphic Works of the Impressionists,* New York, 1972) catalogs this work under Pissarro No. 192 and indicates that this work was published by Jean Grave in 1898. In this respect, see : R. and E. Herbert *Artists and Anarchism*, Burlington Magazine, November, 1960, p. 473.

110. PISSARRO   Etching in colors (6th State), 1890

111. PISSARRO   Lithograph in colors (2nd State), 1901

112. CAMILLE PISSARRO (1831-1903)

Mendiant et paysanne, circa 1897.
Lithograph on zinc.
11 5/8 x 8 1/2 inches ; 297 x 215 mm.
Signed lower right : «C. Pissarro», titled lower center : «Mendiant et paysanne» and annotated, lower left : «Ep. d'essai No. 3».

Reference :
Delteil 183-II/II.

Notes :

This fine and rare lithograph is printed on a greyish chine appliqué. According to Delteil, there were only two impressions of the Ist State and «5 or 6» proofs of the 2nd State, in which the outline of the bag of the beggar extends beyond his right hand. Delteil describes the «5 or 6» proofs of the 2nd State as being annotated, as this one : «ép. d'essai» and then signed and numbered «with the exception of 3 or 4 proofs» of which two had been in the Tailliardet Collection.

112. PISSARRO Lithograph (2nd State), about 1897

113. **ODILON REDON** (1840-1916)

Dans mon rêve, je vis au ciel un visage de mystère (Im my dream, I saw a mysterious face in the sky), 1885.
Lithograph on chine appliqué.
11 1/2 x 9 3/8 inches ; 291 x 238 mm.
Annotated : «à Mademoiselle Firenne Piraux (?) Souvenir amical» and signed «Odilon Redon».

Reference :
  Mellerio No. 54.

Notes :
  This lithograph is a proof from the suite of six lithographs : *Hommage à Goya* printed by Lemercier et Cie, Paris and published in 50 impressions by L. Dumont, Paris, 1885. There also was a later and rather weaker printing of 25 impressions.

113. REDON   Lithograph, 1885

114. PIERRE AUGUSTE RENOIR (1841-1919)

Enfants jouant à la Balle, 1898-1900.
Lithograph in black on MBM Arches paper.
19 11/16 x 19 7/8 inches ; 500 x 505 mm.

References :
1. Delteil No. 32.
2. Roger-Marx No. 7.
3. Johnson-Vollard No. 111.

Notes :
One of a few trial proofs printed in black before the edition of 200 printed in colors by
A. Clot and published by Ambroise Vollard.

114. RENOIR   Lithograph, 1898-1900

115. AUGUSTE RODIN (1840-1917)

L'Eternel Printemps, 1884.
Bronze.
Height : 9 1/2 inches ; 242 mm.
Signed and stamped with the foundry-mark «F. Barbedienne». In the interior numbered «11».

Notes :
1. Executed in 1884, this bronze is one of 69 casts of this size made by the Barbedienne Foundry between 1884 and 1918.
2. Nineteenth century French art critic Edmond de Goncourt wrote about Rodin : «He was a man who had in his head a mixture of Dante, Michelangelo, Victor Hugo and Delacroix».
3. Arnold Haskell (*French Sculpture*, Bruton, England, 1979) wrote that : «Rodin's contribution to the development of sculpture was to free it from all preconceived formulae, going beyond the realism of his immediate forerunners and yet further from the academic 'corpses' as he called the 19th century Salon's marble figures... Rodin's enduring precept that an artist should be truthful to what he *felt* is powerfully expressed in every one of his works...».

Literature :
1. Ionel Jianou and Céline Goldschneider *Rodin*, Paris, 1967, p. 96 (catalogued), plates 56-57 (illustration of another cast).
2. John Tancock *The Sculpture of A. Rodin*, Philadelphia, 1976, pages 241-247, no. 326 (illustration of another cast).

115. RODIN   Bronze, 1884

116. HENRI «LE DOUANIER» ROUSSEAU (1844-1910)

La Guerre, 1894.
Pen lithograph on orange paper.
8 1/2 x 12 3/4 inches : 214 x 323 mm.

References :

1. Page 25 (reproduced) of *Henri Rousseau*, The Museum of Modern Art in New York and the Art Institute of Chicago, presented by Daniel Catton Rich, 1942.
2. Pages 8 and 9 of : *La Guerre du Douanier Rousseau* by G. Bazin in *Bulletin des Musées de France*, XIe année, no. 2, April, 1946.
3. Reproduced in : *Commandée par Rémy de Gourmont, l'unique lithographie du Douanier Rousseau* by Charles Perussaux in *Les Lettres Françaises,* August 30, 1956.
4. Page 19 of : *Henri Rousseau* by Jean Bouret, Neuchâtel, 1961.
5. Pages 145-147 of : *La Vérité sur le Douanier Rousseau* by Henry Certigny, Paris, 1961.
6. Reproduced as no. 21 in : *Henri Rousseau* by Dora Vallier, Paris, 1961.
7. Reproduced on page 56 of : *Henri Rousseau* by Dora Vallier, Paris, 1979.
8. Pages 360-361 of : *Une Source du Douanier Rousseau* by M-T. Lemoyne de Forges, in *Art de France IV*, Paris, 1964.
9. No. 10 and reproduced in color on page 131 of : *Le Douanier Rousseau*, Galeries Nationales du Grand Palais, September 1984 - January, 1985, Paris.
10. No. 10 and reproduced in color in *Le Douanier Rousseau*, Museum of Modern Art, New York, February-June, 1985.

Notes :

1. This now rare lithograph was published in 1894-1895 in a review called *L'Ymagier*, directed by Rémy de Gourmont and Alfred Jarry.
2. This is the unique graphic work of Rousseau. It is a rather simplified version of a painting, *La Guerre* (War) which was No. 9 in the 1984 Paris and 1985 New York (Museum of Modern Art) Rousseau exhibitions. The painting, belonging to the Paris Musée d'Orsay generally hangs in the Jeu de Paume (RF 1946-1). In the lithograph, as indicated by Charles Perussaux in *Les Lettres Françaises* of August 30, 1956, the sky is considerably more vast than in the painting. On the other hand, the trees in the lithograph are much less important and present less of a decorative effect than in the painting. In addition some of the figures in the lithograph seem to be raising themselves in a last dying gesture while the figures in the painting appear to be dead. Finally, the face of the Child-Destructor is quite different in the lithograph compared to the painting.

116. «LE DOUANIER» ROUSSEAU   Pen lithograph, 1894

117. KER-XAVIER ROUSSEL (1867-1944)

L'Education du Chien, 1893.
Lithograph in colors : edition of 100.
12 7/8 x 7 1/2 inches ; 328 x 190 mm.
Signed, numbered and with the blind-stamp of *L'Estampe Originale* (Lugt 819).

Reference :
  Salamon 10.

Formerly collection :
  Alfred Beurdeley (1847-1919) with his mark (Lugt 421).

117. K-X ROUSSEL   Lithograph in colors, 1893

118. **PAUL SERUSIER** (1863-1927)

La petite anse.
Crayon drawing with gouache.
9 x 13 3/4 inches ; 230 x 350 mm.
Atelier stamp, lower left.

Verso :
    Boutaric-Sérusier Collection stamp.

Reference :
    Boutaric-Sérusier Collection No. 439.

Provenances :
1. Atelier of Paul Sérusier.
2. Madame Paul Sérusier.
3. Mlle Boutaric (friend of the widow of the artist).
4. Vente Boutaric-Sérusier, 1984.

119. **PAUL SERUSIER** (1863-1927)

Sous-bois.
Crayon drawing in three colors.
12 3/8 x 9 1/2 inches ; 315 x 240 mm.
Atelier stamp, lower left.

Verso :
    Boutaric-Sérusier Collection stamp.

Reference :
    Boutaric-Sérusier Collection No. 371.

Provenances :
1. Atelier of Paul Sérusier.
2. Madame Paul Sérusier.
3. Mlle Boutaric (friend of the widow of the artist).
4. Vente Boutaric-Sérusier, 1984.

120. **PAUL SERUSIER** (1863-1927)

Femme en forêt.
Black crayon drawing.
7 1/2 x 6 3/4 inches ; 190 x 170 mm.
Atelier stamp, lower right.

Verso :
    Boutaric-Sérusier Collection stamp.

Reference :
    Boutaric-Sérusier Collection No. 326.

Provenances :
1. Atelier of Paul Sérusier.
2. Madame Paul Sérusier.
3. Mlle Boutaric (friend of the widow of the artist).
4. Vente Boutaric-Sérusier, 1984.

118. SERUSIER Crayon drawing with gouache

119. SERUSIER Crayon drawing in three colors

120. SERUSIER Black crayon drawing

121. PAUL SIGNAC (1863-1935)

Les Bateaux (2nd State), 1895.
Lithograph in colors, with remarque.
9 1/4 x 15 3/4 inches ; 237 x 400 mm.
Numbered in pencil as one of twenty impressions of this state.

Reference :
Kornfeld/Wick 13-II/III.

Notes :
This is a particularly fine impression of one of the twenty proofs of the 2nd State (of three) with «remarque». There followed the 40 impressions of the 3rd State without «remarque». This lithograph was printed by Clot and published by Gustave Pellet.

121. SIGNAC   Lithograph in colors (2nd State), 1895

122.   HENRI DE TOULOUSE-LAUTREC (1864-1901)

Homme assis et cavaliers, circa 1882.
Charcoal drawing.
22 7/8 x 14 3/4 inches ; 580 x 450 mm.

Provenance :
1. Gustave-Lucien Dennery, Paris (Dennerey was a friend of Toulouse-Lautrec at Cormon's atelier).
2. Sale, Paris, Palais Galliers, March 27th, 1962 : no. 99.

Literature :
1. Maurice Joyant, *Henri de Toulouse-Lautrec,* Paris, 1926, vol. II, p. 181 (catalogued among the *18 Fusains*).
2. M.G. Dortu, *Toulouse-Lautrec et son Oeuvre,* New York, 1971, vol. V, no. D.1.912 (reproduced).

Notes :
1. This drawing dates from about 1882 when Toulouse-Lautrec was studying at Cormon's atelier in Paris.
2. Toulouse-Lautrec continually drew and sketched. His schoolbooks already were filled with delightful «croquis». The liveliness and abundance of these early «notations» developed into an extraordinary suppleness of line and contour. Specific traits and movements were grasped by his pen with quick understanding. Carriages, dogs, people and horses were among his favorite, early subjects. In these early works, though influenced by his instructor, the horse painter Rene Princeteau, Toulouse-Lautrec already showed a strong and independant artistic personality.
3. Thadee Natanson (*Un Henri de Toulouse-Lautrec,* Geneva, 1951) has written extensively on Toulouse-Lautrec's early works : «From his childhood until his last day, as long as he was able, Toulouse-Lautrec put nothing above the happiness of drawing» (page 289)... «He knew by heart the appearance and movement of horses. When he contemplated them, he believed strongly in precisely rectifying every detail...» (page 92).

122b.   HENRI DE TOULOUSE-LAUTREC (1864-1901)

Feuille d'étude de cavaliers et de sabots de chevaux, about 1883.
Pen, pencil and india ink drawing.
7 x 11 1/2 inches ; 178 x 292 mm.
With red atelier stamp, lower left.

Reference :
M.G. Dortu *Toulouse-Lautrec et son œuvre,* New York, 1971 : No. D 2, 803, Vol. V.

Exhibited :
Toulouse-Lautrec : Master of Graphic Art, R.S. Johnson International, Fall, 1979, reproduced on page 47.

122. TOULOUSE-LAUTREC Charcoal drawing, about 1882

123. **HENRI DE TOULOUSE-LAUTREC** (1864-1901)

A la Gaieté-Rochechouart, Nicolle en Pierreuse, 1893.
Lithograph : edition of 100.
14 7/16 x 10 1/4 inches ; 367 x 260 mm.
With red monogram stamp (Lugt 1338).

References :
1. Delteil No. 48.
2. Adhémar No. 51.
3. Adriani-Wittrock No. 50.

Note :
This work was reproduced in the December 31, 1893 edition of *L'Escarmouche*.

123. TOULOUSE-LAUTREC   Lithograph, 1893

124. HENRI DE TOULOUSE-LAUTREC (1864-1901)

Judic et Dihau or **L'Essai du Corset**, 1893.
Lithograph : edition of 100.
14 5/8 x 10 1/2 inches ; 372 x 266 mm.
With red monogram stamp (Lugt 1338) and numbered.

References :
1. Delteil No. 56.
2. Adhémar No. 39.
3. Adriani-Wittrock No. 54.

Provenance :
Ex-collection Gross (with stamp).

Notes :
1. This work was published by Kleinmann in an edition of 100.
2. The work was reproduced in L'Escarmouche review of December 10th, 1893.
3. On the left is Désiré Dihau waiting while Anna Judic dresses for a performance.

125. HENRI DE TOULOUSE-LAUTREC (1864-1901)

Au Moulin-Rouge, l'Union Franco-Russe, 1894.
Lithograph : edition of 100.
12 15/16 x 9 3/4 inches ; 328 x 247 mm.
With red monogram stamp (Lugt 1338), numbered and with Sagot drystamp (Lugt 2254).

References :
1. Delteil No. 50.
2. Adhémar No. 53.
3. Adriani-Wittrock No. 52.

Notes :
1. This work was reproduced in *L'Escarmouche* on January 7th, 1894.
2. Adhémar notes that the young worker, here depicted is carrying the newspaper *Paris-Sport* under his arm. When memory of the Franco-Soviet celebration had been forgotten, this lithograph became known also as Paris-Sport.

124. TOULOUSE-LAUTREC   Lithograph, 1893

125. TOULOUSE-LAUTREC   Lithograph, 1894

126. HENRI DE TOULOUSE-LAUTREC (1864-1901)

A l'Opéra : Mme Caron dans Faust, 1894.
Lithograph printed in olive-green : edition of 100.
14 3/8 x 10 1/2 inches ; 364 x 266 mm.
Numbered and with red monogram stamp (Lugt 1338).

References :
1. Delteil No. 49.
2. Adhémar No. 52.
3. Adriani-Wittrock No. 51.

Provenances :
1. Maurice l'Oncle (with his collector's stamp). L'Oncle, one of the most famous collectors of the first half of the twentieth century, was particularly interested in Daumier and Toulouse-Lautrec.
2. Ex-collection Gross (with stamp).

Notes :
1. This work was reproduced in the *L'Escarmouche* review of January 7th, 1894.
2. Rose Caron had retired in 1892 but had been persuaded to return for a special performance of Gounod's Faust in order to raise funds for the erection of a statue of Gounod in Paris.

127. HENRI DE TOULOUSE-LAUTREC (1864-1901)

Au Théâtre-Libre : Antoine dans l'Inquiétude, 1893.
Lithograph : edition of 100.
14 3/4 x 10 1/2 inches ; 375 x 266 mm.
With red monogram stamp and numbered 72 from the edition of 100.

References :
1. Delteil No. 51.
2. Adhémar No. 55.
3. Adriani-Wittrock No. 53.

Notes :
1. This lithograph shows Antoine and Madame Saville in *L'Inquiétude* by J. Perrin and C. Couturier at the *Théâtre Libre*.
2. This lithograph, after being pulled in 100 impressions, was reproduced in *L'Escarmouche* on January 14, 1894.

126. TOULOUSE-LAUTREC   Lithograph, 1893

127. TOULOUSE-LAUTREC   Lithograph, 1894

128. HENRI DE TOULOUSE-LAUTREC (1864-1901)

La Goulue et Valentin, 1894.
Lithograph : edition of 100.
11 3/4 x 9 1/16 inches : 298 x 230 mm.
With red monogram stamp (Lugt 1338).

References :
1. Delteil 71.
2. Adhémar 77.
3. Adriani-Wittrock 99.

Notes :
1. This is the same couple in Toulouse-Lautrec's famous poster *Moulin Rouge : La Goulue*, 1891. Depicted in both the poster and in this lithograph was firstly Louise Weber («La Goulue») who had been born in 1870 and had intended to be a laundress. However, in 1887 at the age of 17, she began dancing at the *Moulin de la Galette*, then at the *Elysée-Montmartre* and the *Jardin de Paris* before arriving at the *Moulin-Rouge* in 1890. In the May 10, 1891 number of *Gil Blas*, there is the often cited description of her dancing technique :

«When she began to dance, her cheeks glowed, her unruly locks opened up, her arms rose, her legs swung up, beating the air, threatening the spectators' hats and drawing their attention to the elusive opening of her colorful drawers... as she danced, she alternated the tantalizing arching of her belly with a wonderful wriggling of her hips... slowly concluding her dance... she would allow to be seen, just above her garter, a tiny patch of real, bare skin. From that glimpse of rosy skin, as from molten steel, a scorching ray leaps out to overwhelm the breathless spectators».

La Goulue's partner in this dance scene was Valentin (Jacques Renaudin 1843-1907) who owned a small bar-café in the rue Coquillière and danced in Montmartre without being paid and for his own sheer pleasure. Valentin was described by Gustave Coquiot as «resembling a lamp-post» but who could «waltz at incredible speed and with impeccable rhythm...». La Goulue and Valentin became known as the greatest dancers of their era in Montmartre.
2. After being published by Kleinmann in an edition of 100 impressions before letters, this work afterwards was used as the cover for a waltz named for La Goulue and written by Bosc (with letters : «la Goulue - valse pour piano par A. Bosc»).

128. TOULOUSE-LAUTREC   Lithograph, 1894

129. HENRI DE TOULOUSE-LAUTREC (1864-1901)

Anna Held (Ist State), 1894.
Lithograph : edition of 25 in Ist State.
12 5/8 x 7 7/8 inches ; 320 x 200 mm.
Signed and numbered («No. 25»).

References :
1. Delteil No. 100-I/II.
2. Adhémar No. 112-I/II.
3. Adriani-Wittrock No. 103-I/II.

Notes :
1. This is one of the rare (25) impressions before letters of the Ist State of this famous work. The impressions with letters advertise a play *Toutes ces Dames au Théâtre* in which Anna Held had a role.
2. The singer Anna Held was born in Paris of Polish parents. She became famous singing English and American songs at the *Eldorado.* Adhémar (*Toulouse-Lautrec : His Complete Lithographs and Drypoints,* New York, 1965) refers to Anna Held's long career. In the *Comoedia Illustré*, March 20, 1913, there was written about Anna Held that : «The Americans are mad about her.» After her marriage to Florenz Ziegfield in America, it seems that Anna Held came back to Paris frequently, once to present a lecture on the *chic* of New York.

129. TOULOUSE-LAUTREC   Lithograph (Ist State), 1894

130. HENRI DE TOULOUSE-LAUTREC (1864-1901)

Marcelle Lender debout, 1895.
Lithograph : edition of 15.
13 3/4 x 9 7/16 inches ; 350 x 240 mm.

References :
1. Delteil No. 103.
2. Adhémar No. 134.
3. Adriani-Wittrock No. 119.

Notes :
This is one of the 15 impressions in black and white printed for Kleinmann. Delteil notes an additional 12 impressions with the addition of some touches of color lithography.

131. HENRI DE TOULOUSE-LAUTREC (1864-1901)

Luce Myres, de face, 1895.
Lithograph : edition of 20.
12 15/16 x 9 3/4 inches ; 328 x 247 mm.
With red monogram stamp (Lugt 1338) and numbered «No. 16».

References :
1. Delteil 125.
2. Adhémar 139.
3. Adriani-Wittrock 125.

Notes :
This extremely rare lithograph shows Luce Myres in a revival of *La Perichole* at the Théâtre des Variétés. It was published by Kleinmann in an edition of only 20.

130. TOULOUSE-LAUTREC   Lithograph, 1895

131. TOULOUSE-LAUTREC   Lithograph, 1895

132. HENRI DE TOULOUSE-LAUTREC (1864-1901)

La Passagère (Ist State), 1896.
Lithograph in colors : edition of 100 in Ist State.
23 5/16 x 16 inches ; 608 x 407 mm.
Signed and numbered.

References :
1. Delteil 366-I/II.
2. Adhémar No. 188-I/II.
3. Adriani-Wittrock No. 145-I/II.

Notes :
1. A superb impression with very fresh colors.
2. This lithograph, with letters added, later was used as a poster for the Salon des Cent exhibition:
3. The subject was a young woman whom Toulouse-Lautrec, accompanied by his friend Maurice Guibert, had met on a boat going south from Le Havre to Bordeaux. In Bordeaux, Toulouse-Lautrec refused te leave the boat, desiring to accompany the young lady still further on her journey (her eventual destination having been to rejoin her husband in Dakar). Having arrived in Lisbon, Guibert and Toulouse-Lautrec finally were persuaded to disembark. As the story goes, Toulouse-Lautrec apparently never was able to fin out the exact name of the young lady and she has eternally become known as either La Passagère or the Passenger from Cabin 54.

132. TOULOUSE-LAUTREC   Lithograph in colors (Ist State), 1896

133. HENRI DE TOULOUSE-LAUTREC (1864-1901)

Elles : La Clownesse assise, 1896.
Lithograph in colors : edition of 100.
20 1/2 x 15 3/4 inches ; 520 x 400 mm.
With Pellet's paraphe, lower right.

References :
1. Delteil No. 180.
2. Adhémar No. 201.
3. Adriani-Wittrock No. 178.

Notes :
1. A super impression with very fresh colors.
2. Colta Feller Ives (*The Great Wave : The Influence of Japanese Woodcuts on French Prints*, The Metropolitain Museum of Art, New York, 1974, page 94) feels that Toulouse-Lautrec may have picked this particular subject for the first of the *Elles* plates in order to emphasize the oriental nature of both the subject and his treatment of it. Taken from the Moulin Rouge, this scene shows the clowness who had changed her name from «Chahut-Chaos» (a description of her acrobatic dancing act) to the more oriental «Cha-U-Kao». Ives notes that the clowness is :

> unexpectedly posed like one of Hokusai's nimble acrobats, her silhouetted arms and legs interlocked in a splendid example of the Japanese arabesque. She occupies a space ruled by Japanese perspective : the floor tilted up, the background defined by strips of color. The spattered «crachis» recreate the glittering surfaces of Utamaro's prints, which were sometimes sprinkled with brass powder over yellow grounds... The luscious pinks and yellows of the Clownesse and elsewhere in *Elles* were probably also inspired by Utamaro's woodcuts... In both how he made his prints and what he put in them Lautrec learned from the Japanese... Lautrec, who was inspired by the overall formal effects of the Japanese woodcut - its color, line, and patterning - fortuitously recognized a graphic character close to his own temperament and perfectly suited to the lithographic medium. No other western artist so completely adopted the Japanese woodcut for his own purposes.

133. TOULOUSE-LAUTREC   Lithograph in colors, 1896

134. HENRI DE TOULOUSE-LAUTREC (1864-1901)

Petite Fille Anglaise (Miss Dolly, Star, Le Havre), 1899.
Lithograph : on wove paper, one of about nine impressions.
8 3/4 x 6 7/8 inches ; 220 x 175 mm.
Signed in pencil and dedicated «à Calmese».

References :
1. Delteil No. 145.
2. Adhémar No. 367.
3. Adriani-Wittrock No. 392.

Notes :
1. Delteil records only nine impressions of this extremely rare lithograph.
2. After his discharge from the Madrid-les-Bains asylum in July of 1899, Toulouse-Lautrec left Paris to convalesce in the countryside. Finally, he ended up in Le Havre, where he took rooms in a sailor's tavern called *The Star*. Here he did drawings and paintings of the tavern's customers and entertainers. He also did three now extremely rare lithographs, including this one of *Miss Dolly, a Young English Girl*. Another of these lithographs, *La Chanson du Matelot-Miss X in the Alabamah Coons*, shows another English girl singer who is dressed up as a sailor.
3. This lithograph is dedicated : «à Calmèse». Edouard Calmèse was the owner of a stable in Le Havre in the Rue de la Fontaine, where Toulouse-Lautrec kept his poney Philibert.
4. This work is quite close to a watercolor (in reverse) reproduced on page 203 of : Maurice Joyant *Henri de Toulouse-Lautrec*, Paris, 1926-1927.

134. TOULOUSE-LAUTREC   Lithograph, 1899

135. **HENRI DE TOULOUSE-LAUTREC** (1864-1901)

Le Jockey, 1899-1900.
Lithograph in colors : edition of 100.
20 1/16 x 14 3/16 inches ; 510 x 360 mm.

References :
1. Delteil No. 279.
2. Adhémar No. 365.
3. Adriani-Wittrock No. 356.

Notes :
1. A superb impression with very fresh colors.
2. There were 100 impressions in black and white only, and then 100 impressions in color, including this one. Delteil mistakenly indicates that the edition in black and white was of 10 rather than 100 impressions. Delteil notes that this lithograph was the only one by Toulouse-Lautrec to have been published by Pierrefort. This work was to have been part of a serie on *Les Courses*, which project was never realized.

135. TOULOUSE-LAUTREC   Lithograph in colors, 1899-1900

136. JULES JACQUES VEYRASSAT (1828-1893)

Marché de Chevaux.
Watercolor over pencil.
10 x 14 3/4 inches ; 254 x 375 mm.
Signed lower right.

Note :
Besides his fine watercolors, Veyrassat, within the Barbizon School, also was known as a fine etcher.

136. VEYRASSAT   Watercolor and pencil

137. JACQUES VILLON (1875-1963)

Danseuse espagnole (undescribed lst State), 1899.
Aquatint in colors.
20 x 13 3/4 inches ; 508 x 357 mm.
Annotated in the hand of Villon «1er état» (lst State).

References :
1. Auberty et Perussaus No. 5.
2. Ginestet & Pouillon No. E. 23.

Notes :
1. An undescribed and apparently unique lst State of this work : before the addition of two lines in drypoint by the leg of the chair on the left and before the use of the green color found in the final state. Annotated in the hand of Villon «1er état» (lst State).
2. Ginestet & Pouillon (*Jacques Villon - Les Estampes et les Illustrations : Catalogue Raisonné*, Paris, 1979) do not seem to know of this lst State impression. They do note certain «color differences» in the edition which, according to the numbering, would appear to be twenty-five. This color aquatint appears to be far rarer than the apparent edition number would seem to indicate. The *Danseuse espagnole* was not in the 1954 Paris exhibit at Louis Carré's : *Jacques Villon : Oeuvre Gravé* nor was it in *Jacques Villon : Collection Louis Carré* Drouot Rive-Gauche vente of 1978. This work also was not found in the Ludwig Charell Villon Collection offered at Drouot in Paris in 1967 nor was it included in the *Hommage à Jacques Villon* exhibit at Sagot-Le Garrec in Paris in 1975 nor was it included in the major *Jacques Villon* retrospective at the Musée des Beaux-Arts, Rouen and at the Grand Palais, Paris, both in 1975. The *Danseuse espagnole* also was not found among the collection of Madame Marcel Duchamp : *Important Ensemble de Gravures Originales de Jacques Villon* offered by Ader-Picard-Tajan in Paris in 1976. This work was not included in the Art Institute of Chicago's retrospective Villon exhibit in 1976 nor was it found in the retrospective *Jacques Villon Grafiek* held at the Rijksmuseum in Amsterdam in 1984. To our knowledge, only five impressions of Villon's *Danseuse espagnole* have come to the fore over the past thirty years. One of these is a trial proof in dark brown, belonging to the Museum of Modern Art, New York (exhibited as cat. no. 4 in : *Jacques Villon : His Graphic Art*, The Museum of Modern Art, New York, 1953 and again exhibited as cat. no. 3 : *Jacques Villon : Master of Graphic Art*, Museum of Fine Arts, Boston, 1964). Secondly, there is the no. 13 in *Jacques Villon*, Bibliothèque Nationale, Paris, 1959. Thirdly, there is the «bon à tirer», dedicated to Delâtre, from a private collection and also exhibited at the Museum of Fine Arts in Boston in 1964 (cat. no. 4). Finally, there is the impression numbered 17/25 and exhibited as cat. no. 3 in : *Jacques Villon : Master of Graphic Art*, R.S. Johnson International, Chicago, 1967 and exhibited again as catalog no. 5 in : *Hommage to Jacques Villon*, R.S. Johnson International, Chicago, 1975-1976. In conclusion, the above four impressions (at least two of which are proofs : we have not examined the impression of the Bibliothèque Nationale) plus the present lst State trial proof appear to be the only known impressions of this work. All this would seem to indicate that either Villon only pulled a few impressions of an edition apparently meant to be twenty-five or else that, since 1899, somehow a major part of this edition has been lost or destroyed.
3. There is a watercolor-study for this work which had been exhibited as no. 141 and reproduced on page 38 of : *Jacques Villon : Master of Graphic Art*, Museum of Fine Arts, Boston, 1964. This work from the collection of Benjamin Sonnenberg was dispersed after Sonnenberg's death.

137. VILLON   Aquatint in colors (undescribed Ist State), 1899

138. EDOUARD VUILLARD (1868-1940)

La Prairie, circa 1898.
Colored pastels.
10 7/16 x 10 inches ; 265 x 254 mm.
With stamped initials (Lugt 909a).

Note :
    A fine example from Vuillard's late Nabi period.

138. VUILLARD   Colored pastels, about 1898

139. EDOUARD VUILLARD (1868-1940)

Intérieur aux Tentures Roses I, 1899.
Lithograph in colors.
14 x 11 inches ; 355 x 280 mm.

Reference :
  Roger-Marx No. 36.

Notes :
  1. A particularly beautifully colored impression from the edition of 100, included in *Paysages et Intérieurs,* published by Ambroise Vollard in 1899.
  2. Colta Feller Ives (*The Great Wave : The Influence of Japanese Woodcuts on French Prints,* The Metropolitain Museum of Art, New York, 1974) notes that (page 68) :

> The evocative, almost spiritual rendering of life in much of Vuillard's art parallels the interest of many Japanese prints, especially those of Harunobu, which depict quiet interiors and simple figures bathed in nostalgia and a vague melancholy...

Ives goes on to note that (page 71) :

> The prominnent role of decorative patterns in *Landscapes and Interiors* links Vuillard's prints to the Japanese, which rely on the sumptuous patterning of fabrics for much for their attractiveness. Vuillard, like so many of the Ukiyo-e printmakers, was part of the fabric-designing tradition. An though he was not, like some Japanese artists, skilled in textile handicrafts, his uncle, the fabric-designer and his mother the dressmaker had filled their apartment with the figured stuffs that prompted a confusion of patterns in Vuillard's work...

139. VUILLARD   Lithograph in colors, 1899

140. EDOUARD VUILLARD (1868-1940)

La Pâtisserie, 1899.
Lithograph in colors.
14 x 10 5/8 inches ; 355 x 270 mm.

Reference :
Roger-Marx No. 41.

Notes :
A particularly beautifully colored impression from the edition of 100, included in *Paysages et Intérieurs*, published by Ambroise Vollard in 1899.

141. EDOUARD VUILLARD (1868-1940)

Intérieur à la Suspension, 1899.
Lithograph in colors.
13 3/4 x 11 inches ; 350 x 280 mm.

Reference :
Roger-Marx No. 35.

Notes :
A particularly beautifully colored impression from the edition of 100, included in *Paysages et Intérieurs*, published by Ambroise Vollard in 1899.

140. VUILLARD Lithograph in colors, 1899

141. VUILLARD Lithograph in colors, 1899

Fig. 4 - GÉRICAULT (cat. no. 66)   Lithograph (2nd State), 1822

Addendum
Selected Notes on the History
of Nineteenth Century France

1795-1799 **The Directory.** In this period, there was a gradual increase in influence of the Army. Napoléon Bonaparte was appointed to lead the French Army of Italy and the Alps.

The return of Bonaparte from Egypt brought to France apparently the one man capable of finishing the war, reorganizing the government and exploiting the gains of ten years of revolution. It also was Bonaparte who perhaps best understood that the Revolution could only be brought to a successful conclusion, through some form of military dictatorship.

1799-1804 **The Consulate.** Napoléon Bonaparte, who had been First Consul of France, was elected in 1802 to be «Consul for Life». This election, in the form of a referendum, established an autocracy upon the basis of universal suffrage. In 1802, three of Napoléon's greatest accomplishments were celebrated in one ceremony at Notre-Dame in Paris. These accomplishments were : the Concordat (agreement with the Chruch) ; the accord of Amiens, resulting in peace in Europe ; and the establishing of Napoléon as «Consul for Life». Two years later, Napoléon was designated Emperor and in 1805 also as King of Italy.

1804-1814	**The First Empire.** Napoléon divorced Josephine. Napoléon embarked on a series of battles with the principle aim being to obtain complete control of all continental ports and capitals. This would have resulted in English ships and goods being excluded from Europe. The battle of Trafalgar (1805) ruined these plans on the sea. On the Continent, however, Napoléon achieved one success after another. After a rather lucky victory over the Russians at Friedland, he concluded the treaty of Tilsit with the Emperor Alexander I in 1807. This agreement with Russia gradually broke down however through the system which deprived Russia of British goods without giving Russia any compensation in French markets. In 1812, deciding to abandon diplomacy for war, Napoléon embarked on another Russian campaign. When Napoléon was forced to retreat from Moscow, the whole Napoleonic empire fell apart. This was aided by the Germans who had been waiting for the chance to liberate themselves from the French «liberators».
1814-1815	**The First Restoration** marked the return of the Bourbons in the person of Louis XVIII, a brother of Louis XVI. A constitutional monarchy was established, with a bicameral parliamentary system after the English model. In 1815, however, Napoleon suddenly returned from Elba and, with the support of the Grande Armée, marched northwards successfully against the Prussian Army in Brussels. Napoléon marched on in order to attempt to completely destroy the army of Wellington, Wellington's army resisted strongly and the Prussians, under Blucher, came to the aid of the British. After his return for «The Hundred Days», Napoléon was completely routed at Waterloo, abdicated four days later and on July 8, 1815, Louis XVIII re-entered Paris.
1815-1830	**The Second Restoration.** Thoroughly disillusioned by Napoléon's «One Hundred Days» and now punished by the rest of Europe, France turned more sharply to the right politically and elected an extremely royalist government. Louis XVIII, on the contrary, seemed to realize that an ultra royalist government could not govern. In 1816, he dissolved the Government and the new elections gave the power back to the Constitutionalists. In the period which followed much of the constructive work of the Restoration was accomplished ; finances were brought into order and the occupying forces finally left France completely by 1818. However, when in 1820 revolutions broke out in various parts of Europe, Louis XVIII began to have second thoughts about his liberal policies and the royalists again became ascendant. After the death of Louis XVIII, his brother Charles X was monarch from 1824 until 1830. Charles X gradually found himself under increasing difficulties. These came to a head in 1830 with three ordinances : dissolution of chamber of deputies ; abolition of freedom of press ; and the electorate was abolished with the exception of about 25,000 landed proprietors. After strikes and barricades, the people's insurrection triumphed. After the rejection of the Bourbons, rather surprisingly the head of the Government was still another nobleman, Louis-Philippe who now was acclaimed as a citizen-king and the result of the revolution.
1830-1848	**The July Monarchy : Louis Philippe.** Basically the revolution of 1830 appeared to be a victory of the bourgeoisie over the aristocracy. Louis-Philippe became not Philippe VII, King of France, but Louis-Philippe King of the French. This was a period of unrest in France. This was partially because of economic problems, but also because of a general disagreement as to the purpose of the 1830 revolution. Some wished a swing to the right while others thought increasing liberty was what should be the Government's objective. The developing industrialization also posed a problem for the quality of life in the increasingly crowded cities. A turning point in the reign of Louis-Philippe came with the economic crisis of 1846 coming from the failure of the potato and wheat crops in a great part of northern and western Europe. An agricultural depression was soon followed by an industrial depression. To this was added a financial crisis caused by over-speculation in the first French railways. The marriage of the King's son Antoine with the infanta Maria-Luisa Fernanda (the heiress presumptive of Spain) politically upset the British and was the final blow destroying the French-British entente. Many of France's problems were blamed on Louis-Philippe's minister Guizot. The king finally dismissed Guizot. However, in the midst of all this, on

February 23, 1848, troops fired on a crowd of demonstrators. Suddenly tempers flared, an armed insurrection developed and the king fled to England where he died three years later.

1848-1852 **The Second Republic.** For a majority, the revolution was a political change : monarchy was replaced with a free democratic government (voters increased from 200,000 to 9,000,000). A minority also hailed a social and economic transformation. There was an uneasy alliance between two elements. Basically France was still conservative : Radicals and Socialists only held 100 out of 876 seats. At this time, extremists in Paris stirred up the workers who arose but then were defeated. In the election which followed, the winner was Prince Louis Napoléon. This finally resulted in the complete overthrow of the Republic, for Louis Napoléon felt his mission was to restore the empire. In a December 1-2, 1851 coup d'état, Louis Napoléon dissolved the parliament.

1852-1870 **The Second Empire.** The coup d'état was widely popular. A plebicite approved it with an overwhelming majority and Louis Napoléon became Napoléon III. This was a period of great French economic development, of much more industrial and financial power. Overall, however, France still remained essentially a land of artisans and peasants. Napoléon III's reign was splenderous, beginning with the sumptuous court fetes around the 1853 monarch's marriage with a Spanish countess, Eugenia de Montijo. In the political world, the «German question» in the 1860's gradually became the crucial issue for the balance of European power. The fact that France was obliged to accept unification of northern Germany under Prussian hegemony, without any compensation, was universally seen as a grave blow to French influence and prestige. Added to all this was the failure of the Mexican expedition with the execution of Maximilien in Mexico.

July, 1870 **Franco-German War.** The French Government declared war on Germany. In the following war, the French armies were outgeneraled, outnumbered and outmaneuvred. There was an overwhelming defeat of Marshall MacMahon at Sedan. On September 4, there was a bloodness revolution in Paris. The empire ended and the Third Republic was declared.

Until 1900 **The Third Republic.** In 1871, Thiers was appointed chief of the executive of the new French Republic. There was a treaty with Germany to which France was to pay an indemnity of 5,000,000,000 Francs. France gave up Alsace and Lorraine. Finally, France agreed to allow German troops to make a formal, triumphal march through Paris. This led to the outbreak of «The Commune» which then was mercilessly repressed. By having Bismark agree to an earlier withdrawal of troops in proportion to the early payment of the indemnity, Thiers allowed France to be free of the Germans by September, 1873. There followed a period of economic recovery. The growth of moderate republicanism and the obvious hopelessness of royalism ensured support for a conservative republic.
In 1873, Thiers was suceeded by Marshall MacMahon who was given the «presidency of the republic» for seven years. After three years of growth, there followed a drepression with the farmers the main losers. The index of prices fell from 159 in 1873 to 130 in 1879. There were bad harvests in 1878 and 1879. Without the industrial districts of Alsace and the metalurgical industries of Lorraine, French industry ran into difficulties. In 1875, there was a new constitution in which legislative power was vested in a National Assembly consisting of a senate and a chamber of deputies. At this time, more than half of France still lived by agriculture. It was in this period that Gambetta, the most dynamic leader of the Republicans until his death in 1882, conceived of the idea of a democracy composed of peasant proprietors and small businessmen. Another element of importance was the growing influence of labor organizations in French politics. The French found themselves subject to many internal differences : some of these were between Royalists and Republicans, others between clericals and anti-clericals. These problems became more intense because of the Dreyfus case of 1894-1899. Dreyfus, a French officer of Jewish descent, had been accused of giving military secrets to the Germans. Emile Zola, in his famous letter to the President of the Republic, *J'accuse*, alleged an army conspiracy to

condemn Dreyfus despite his innocence. The rights and wrongs of Dreyfus as an individual gradually dropped out of sight : Nationalists, clericals and right-wingers tended to be anti-Dreyfusard ; while republicans, anti-clericals and Socialists tended to be Dreyfusard. In 1889, Dreyfus was pardonned because shown to be innocent. It was on this note that the political history of 19th Century France terminated. The Dreyfus affaire, which became known as the «affaire», was a symptom of France's political instability and social capriciousness at the turn of the century.

In a period of seventy years, (1870-1940) France saw the rise and fall of no less than seventy different governments, thirty-nine of which rose and fell between 1870 and 1900. The cause of this instability came from the constant fragmenting of the various political parties. This was already clear in 1879 with the apparent victory of the Republican party, which had won majorities in both the senate and the chamber. In this very year of victory, the Republican party split in two halves with moderate and conservative wings led by Gambetta and Jules Ferry (who became known as the Opportunists) while a Radical wing was led by men like Georges Clémenceau. 1879 also was the year of the formation of the Socialist Labor party. Like the Republicans, the Socialist Labor party soon split up between the more extreme Marxists and the Opportunists, or «Possibilists». The instability of the parties of the left was matched among the parties on the right. The Rolyalists' attempt at unification failed and there was a split between the Legitimists and the Orleanists. Finally, the Bonapartists remained a force able to elect 75 seats in the chamber of 1876. In addition, the power accorded to the clergy split through all the political action philosophies. With so many factions and parties, France could only be governed by coalition governments for the last thirty years of the 19th century. The same political instability, for similar reasons, was to extend through the first forty years of the twentieth century.

Fig. 5 - TOULOUSE-LAUTREC (cat. no. 122b)   Drawing, about 1883

Printed in France
Imp. LECERF - ROUEN
1985